NUCLEATION

in

Papua New Guinea Cultures

INTERNATIONAL MUSEUM OF CULTURES

Publication Number 23

C. Henry Bradley
Series Editor

William R. Merrifield
General Editor
Academic Publications Coordinator

NUCLEATION

in

Papua New Guinea Cultures

Marvin K. Mayers

and

Daniel D. Rath

Editors

International Museum of Cultures
Dallas, Texas
1988

Cover illustration and design by Ruth Hara.

Copies of this and other publications of the International Museum of Cultures may be obtained from:

International Museum of Cultures
7500 West Camp Wisdom Road
Dallas, Texas 75236

Contents

Preface

"Back to basics" is a theme in contemporary education. As more and more young people arrive at the threshold of graduate education (let alone undergraduate) with marginal reading and writing skills, more emphasis on these matters at earlier grade or levels is increasingly necessary. So it is in Anthropology. At a time when universities are graduating increasing numbers of professionals, basic analytical skills are called for to provide adequate foundations for the study of cultural and linguistic metaphor and symbolism, mediation within culture, and of sociolinguistics in general. When called upon to run a workshop for field linguists in Papua New Guinea, I went back to the basics of social anthropology: function, structure-function, and structuralism. I discovered that long-term field workers need the conceptual nucleation that such studies provide and that rookie field researchers need the solid foundation of such studies upon which to base their insights.

The Key Concept

One technique I presented was to have each student identify one cultural aspect which helps define or conceptualize the whole of a culture. This approach is perhaps most recently conceived as "Isolation of a Key Concept" (Bastien 1978).

Social Theory

Durkheim's social contract, also called the social consciousness, and paraphrased by me as "what goes on between two to make new," was my starting point. This is an underlying social dynamic that sees societies as the product of social interaction and individuals within the society as bearers of (and themselves creators of) the cultural expression of the society. His concept of the whole being more than the sum total of the parts allows us to see any group involvement as a dynamic process rather than as a static situation.

Malinowski's concept of *function* focuses on the human responses to basic needs which results in the development of social institutions. To meet the needs related to social consciousness, metabolism, reproduction, bodily comforts, safety, movement, growth, and health, societies develop institutions of commissariat, kinship, shelter, protection, activities, training, and hygiene. Abraham Maslow considers these as a hierarchy of needs which human beings seek to meet to achieve fulfillment in life. His hierarchy begins at the lowest level with needs similar to Malinowski's and progresses via physiological needs, to safety needs, to belongingness and love needs, to esteem needs, to self-actualization needs to the maximum fulfillment of life expressed in aesthetic needs.

Radcliffe-Brown extends the concept of function into a structure-function model which he expresses as "the part in relation to the whole": the part in the whole being the *structure,* and the relationship of the part to the whole being the *function.* This concept is developed into a network of social relations lying at the foundation of culture and concomitantly the expression of that culture. For convenience, the workshop participants classified various functions as social (interaction, control, stratification, education, etc.), economic (garden, trade relationship, market exchange, etc.), political (executive, legislative, judicial), religious (worship, mediation, appeasement, control, etc.). Radcliffe-Brown's concept of equilibrium theory allows one to see culture as originating in equilibrium, losing this balance through various stresses and strains, and finally establishing a new equilibrium which in turn is forced again into a condition of disequilibrium. Society can be studied in this way to discover the forces of change operating upon it and the results of such change.

Julian Stewart conceptualized five levels of sociocultural integration beginning with the least complex and moving in stages to the most complex. Applying his model to the Papua New Guinea situation, the field worker needs to be aware of and to work with three major levels of integration: the village, the national, and the international levels.

The village level has been the one of primary development producing the foundation for sociocultural integration in the country, i.e., the basis for personal security. Numerous social forces have damaged or destroyed village-level integration including: business interests, cash cropping, mission, Western-style education, the English language, a money economy, etc. These same social forces and others as well will legislate against a restoration of village-level integration. Social equilibrium will need to be restored at some other level or between levels of integration.

The national level of integration is now being developed with concepts of national high schools, national language, national government, national identity, national electrification, etc. The leap from village to national level seems almost unmanageable for a village-level person. An intermediate level between village and nation seems to be lacking. Where there is such a development, Pidgin becomes the medium of communication.

A simple example may serve to define more clearly integration at a village level as distinct from integration at a national level. One white expatriate in a village will give whatever he has to the villager, another will only sell it. Both are "successful" in the eyes of the villagers, very much respected and very much sought after. I would suggest that the first is responding to a village level of integration. The people have shared with each other throughout the village history. It is only natural that an outsider enter quickly into the mutual exchange system and do his part by giving. In return, the villagers are usually willing to serve him in a variety of ways: walk for mail, maintain the airstrip, build his house, etc. The second is responding to the new emerging national level of integration. The villagers have felt the pressures of it in their own villages: presence of government representatives, presence of other expatriates, opportunity to develop a cash crop, formal education, etc. They have experienced it outside the village and brought reports back to the village. Members of their own village have gone out and stayed out, making a living in government and business. Some of the villagers have begun to realize the value of emergence into this new level of integration and are responsive to the outsider, recognizing his presence (and practice of selling goods) as an important step into the larger world.

There are two aspects of the national level of sociocultural integration that need to be clarified in light of the Papua New Guinea experience. On one hand business interests: stores, industries, cash crop trade relationships (coffee, tea, potatoes, vegetables, etc.) have sprung up to point the way to an integration at this level around a money economy: wages, cash capital investment, purchase of needed goods and services. This is reflected in and emerging from commercial centers such as Moresby, Rabaul, Lae, etc. It is being reinforced wherever expatriates participate in the social, religious, and economic opportunities granted them by officialdom. On the other hand, government interests extend a vast array of social aids, welfare, grants and subsidies to the villagers who welcome this as an expression of goodwill in light of their socialization within the village level of integration. However, such goodwill is difficult to reciprocate because of the size and impersonal nature of government, but the villagers soon learn it does not need to be reciprocated. They thus have found themselves within a money economy without the urgency to seek a workingman's wage. These two forces of integration continue to exist in tension, with some nationals seeking to steer the nation into a new emerging international level of integration, by pressing toward socialism or even communism to reinforce the village-level integration, and others steering it toward Western-type capitalism to reinforce the national level.

Lévi-Strauss's concept of binary opposition encourages the detailing of the structure of culture as a series of oppositions which can be studied

within a culture or across cultures to reflect the transformation dynamic of
the structure at any one point in time and through time. A transformation
in his sense is a reversal or some rejuxtaposition of parts of the whole
producing a change in structure.

His concept of *model* is especially useful when one is seeking both to
understand a culture and to be able to think beyond and anticipate, or
predict, behavior that expresses that culture. To quote Lévi-Strauss:

> First, the structure exhibits the characteristics of a system. It is made up of
> several elements, none of which can undergo a change without effecting
> changes in all the other elements.

> Second, for any given model there should be a possibility of ordering a se-
> ries of transformations resulting in a group of models of the same type.

> Third, the above properties make it possible to predict how the model will
> react if one or more of its elements are submitted to certain modifications.

> Finally, the model should be constituted so as to make immediately intel-
> ligible all the observed facts (1967:271–72).

A linear version of the broader Lévi-Strauss model is:

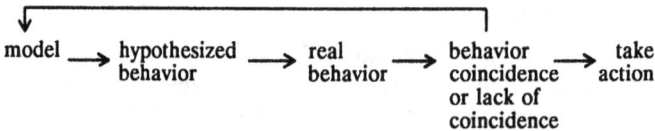

model $\longrightarrow$ hypothesized behavior $\longrightarrow$ real behavior $\longrightarrow$ behavior coincidence or lack of coincidence $\longrightarrow$ take action

Return to model if no coincidence.

The "big man" concept is studied by **Dan Rath** in terms of a universal
(to Papua New Guinea) concept which is then compared with a local or
Mengen, New Britain, concept. The big man strives to fulfill this role
through the accumulation of wealth and the creation of obligations toward
himself in a creditor/debtor relationship. He is a dominant instrument of
social control by demonstrating that he has the skills that command respect. Such control is exercised to maintain cultural traits and patterns of
the past, and thus results in conservatism. He exercises this influence by
means of the traditional "father-of-the-village" role. He thus insures village prosperity, good crops, sound health, fair political dealings, and
peace with the spirits of the supernatural world.

Craig Throop and Mike Fullingim discuss various functions of the pig,
more generally among Melanesians and specifically within the Kaulong
group of New Britain and the Wiru of the mainland. The pig highlights
most, if not all, of the important values within Melanesian culture. These
include the need for food, mediums of exchange, the importance of good
social relationships, the role of the big man in the village-oriented society,
and the importance of relating properly to the spirit world. The pig is thus

a valuable point of reference for describing some of the deeper meanings of Melanesian cultures.

Dean and **Dianne Moore** studied the continued use of traditional shell money among the Duke of York peoples of New Britain. The *diwaara* functions as an object of mediation of relationships between individuals, between clans, and between humans and the spirit world. Thus it is valued for more than money even though it is still used in money-based exchanges. In effect, *diwaara* allows society to run smoothly with good relationships guaranteed by the exchange and distribution of *diwaara*. The "big man," who is found throughout Papua New Guinea society, is the one who possesses the most *diwaara*. Education (in the knowledge and skills society wants its young people to have) is centered in the use and distribution of this traditional shell money. It is required for initiation into the secret society without which knowledge and experience a young man is unable to become a responsible member of his community. It is also necessary to learn skills from a specialist—skills a young person needs to have to succeed in his community and gain his own supply of *diwaara*.

Takashi Manabe reveals how *mami* (yam) as conceptual female, forms a dynamic opposition with ceremonial man as conceptual male to achieve social integration among the Kwange of the Sepik River. Nucleating social relationships are established between two hamlets, thus forming the foundation of an exchange system. *Mami* is exchanged between the two hamlets in a cycle moving from the Tambaran house (ceremonial center) and the garden. The Tambaran house is a place where men and *mami* can receive special power and secret knowledge from the spirits called *masalai* and from ancestral spirits as well. Garden is a place where empowered *mami* is planted by empowered men using secret knowledge they received in the Tambaran house to generate fertility in *mami*. Most of the empowered *mami* that comes from the Tambaran house is consumed by human beings and pigs in expectation of fertility. Thus the power of the spirit world is communicated through men planting, handling, and eating *mami* within the ceremonial context of the Tambaran house as male.

Ron Lewis studying the Saniyo-Hiowe group of the Sepik River explicates a primary opposition of kinship as the cohesive force in Saniyo-Hiyowe society and taboo as the ingredient providing the society with foundational solidarity. Members of this social group interact in four overlapping yet distinct types of relationships: consanguineal, affinal, friendship, and ancestral. Taboos restrict the intake of food, guide one's relationships with others as well as one's relationships with the spirit world. The two systems operate together to control the behavior of individuals within the society.

Judy Kennedy studied the feasts in which Saibai Islanders participate. These people are speakers of a West Torres Strait dialect in Australia which in reality is both geographically and culturally close to Papua New Guinea. There are two kinds of feasts depending upon whether formal invitations are extended or not. Open feasts may be attended by anyone in the community. Closed feasts are attended by the extended family only. The feasts all involve the expenditure of a great deal of money, time, and effort since each member of the society becomes obligated to provide each of the feasts for community as well as family. Consequently, three areas of social stress are developing. First, the cost of a feast continues to rise with total obligations consuming an inordinate amount of an individual's income (some estimates go as much as 90 percent of one's income). Second, normal life-cycle rituals that may be delayed are postponed, e.g., marriage, since the financial means of a family are expended on those that cannot be postponed, e.g., funeral and tombstone opening. Third, educated young people, sensing the threat of such inflation and increase of obligation are reticent to return home due to the heavy burden of such practices on their present and future economic well-being. Irrespective of these areas of stress, however, the people of Saibai see the feasts as worthwhile since they provide a sense of fulfillment and well-being in so many areas of their lives.

Rod Kennedy suggests that, for the Torres Strait people living on Sabaai Island in Australia, the intermediary is one of the key social roles maintaining the stability of the society. Open expression of conflicting wishes is socially unacceptable except between very close relatives. The intermediary acts as initial go-between preventing sudden accidental expression of sharply contrary wishes. The need to avoid any denial of unity is fulfilled by close adherence to expected role behavior. The mediator filters interpersonal communications so that, by the time the parties for whom he mediates are in direct contact, he will have influenced them to the point where the views they express to each other directly are mutually compatible within the context of their respective status-defined roles. There is a great deal of dependence on interpersonal mediation to accomplish any kind of transaction with outsiders and with persons perceived to be of higher rank than the initiator of the transaction.

References

Bastien, Joseph W. 1978. *Mountain of the Condor: Metaphor and Ritual in an Andean Ayllin.* (American Ethnological Society, Monograph 64) St. Paul: West Publishing.

Lévi-Strauss, Claude. 1967. *Structural Anthropology.* (Anchor Books) Garden City, NY:Doubleday.

The Big Man in Mengen Society

Daniel D. Rath

Introduction

The "big man" is the community leader in Melanesia and as such integrates and vitalizes the social experience of the community. Read (1946), Chowning (1977), and Oliver (1955) discuss the qualities that a big man should have. Sahlins (1963) characterizes the big man in contrast with the "chief" of Polynesian society. Salisbury (1964) and Finney (1968) are concerned with the big man's role as outside government and the enticements of the business world enter his society. Finney, along with Burns et al. (1972), elaborates on the big man as achiever. F. Panoff (1969, 1970) and M. Panoff (1970) have studied the Mengen culture to some degree and reflect upon the role of the *maga tamana* 'father of the village' who functions as the big man in Mengen society.

This paper presents a composite picture of the "big man" and the place he holds within the Melanesian society. The big man concept as *maga tamana* is then described as it is found within Mengen society.[1] Finally,

---

1. The Mengen people live along approximately 100 miles of the southeast coast of the island of New Britain in Papua New Guinea. A group also resides inland from Jacquinot Bay about an eight-hour walk. There are approximately 6000 speakers of Mengen, an Austronesian language of the Mengen language family. An estimated 70 percent of the people are literate, and almost all are bilingual in Tok Pisin (Pidgin). As they are educated, an increasing number are becoming conversant in English. A number of Mengen speakers have become teachers, doctors, lawyers, and government personnel and have entered various other vocations. The Mengen people remain basically a subsistence society with some cash cropping in copra and cacao. Several coconut plantations and a timber company that has recently moved into the area employ a number of Mengen people. Currently (1981) there is a strong movement among the Mengen people and neighboring language groups to secede from the East New Britain Province. The National Executive Council of the Papua New Guinea government has approved this move, but more procedures must follow.

1

the two descriptions are combined to show how the overall Melanesian concept compares and contrasts with the Mengen realization.

The Melanesian Big Man

It is difficult at times to categorize the Melanesian big man concept within the realms of economic, sociopolitical, and religious functions. This reflects upon the Melanesian society's holistic tendencies in its underlying motivations, rendering it difficult to separate one function of the society from another. This difficulty is experienced when seeing the role of the big man as incorporating within it these functions of the society. He plays a vital part in the society. Perhaps for this reason the big man is seen to be what he really is—a "big" (i.e., influential), man.

Qualifications

Read (1946), Chowning (1977), and Oliver (1955) discuss various characteristics of those who may aspire to become a big man. The position is not hereditary; anyone qualifying within each Melanesian society may assume the position. Frequently, however, the big man is the genealogical head of one of the family groups that comprise the clan. He may also train a deputy, often his son, to become his successor. Only if the big man's son shows little interest in succeeding his father would anyone else achieve the top position.

Others see the aspiring big man as having some of the following characteristics: an intense ambition for this high rank, quick intelligence, industriousness, charisma, and an executive ability in his dealings with his fellows. He is diplomatic and a master of nonphysical coercion. Some nonaspirants to the position have been quoted as saying that it is difficult to become a leader, and both dangerous and burdensome to remain one. Old age allows a big man to become less intensive in his activities.

Because the characteristics of the position within one society may not necessarily be the same as that within another, it is impossible to generalize about the big man complex throughout Melanesia. Nevertheless, one common similarity is that he displays a marked tendency to achieve prestige within the community. He feels that he must constantly struggle to achieve such prestige and respect in his own eyes, in those of his peers, and in his whole society in order to prove himself worthy of holding the title of big man.

Economic Influence

Another universal feature of the Melanesian big man is his ability to accumulate surplus wealth beyond his personal needs. This he does by his own initiative and enterprise, thereby gaining for himself a certain amount of prestige and renown. He displays a significant increase in the use and consumption of those goods that his society values while utilizing his capital wisely. In his daily life in the village, however, he will generally not try to reflect a high standard of living. He tries to keep his neighbors from knowing just how much wealth he has. Thus, the Melanesian big man displays wealthy behavior, trying at all times not to display his material wealth.

His manipulation of wealth also affects his society. He shows generosity in dispensing his wealth, yet gives competitively and thereby creates obligations toward himself in a debtor/creditor relationship. He organizes activities of the society that involve the exchange of wealth. As a big man, he must seek control over the valued domains of his society to widen his base of support. He tends to arrange business transactions to his own advantage, thereby mobilizing the wealth of others through his own wealth-control network.

Sociopolitical Influence

As the big man gains economic importance, his prominence can then give him influence in other areas of his society. He is in a position to carefully weigh his own personal eminence against that of the general welfare. He could be called a center man, standing above the masses by his own doing and thus functioning as a vital influence within the social system.

He probably most affects the social system through establishing relationships of loyalty and obligation with many people. Because of his accomplishments, he gains a number of supporters who are generous in praising his achievements and who extend to him the respect due his name and position. He must continually reinforce this personal loyalty, however, by extending generosity, cooperation, geniality, decency, and trustworthiness to those with whom he has close social relationships. Discontent may quickly sever this loyalty if the big man is impersonal and unresponsive toward his supporters.

The big man is definitely seen as an instrument of social control, which he manifests as a leader of the domains and actions of his own immediate village. His real authority generally relates to his own locality, although his fame does allow him to be treated at least with politeness and bountiful hospitality beyond the village. His personal fame will also raise the prestige of members of his family beyond the confines of the village.

Within the political system of Melanesian culture, the big man is almost totally in the executive, rather than the legislative or judicial, role of government. This is understood by visualizing only one big man at the very top who has amassed, and continues to amass, a fund of personal power. His people have allowed him to place himself in a strategically powerful position. Here he can show his interest in the general welfare of his people and demonstrate the skills that command respect. He naturally heads political units which enable him to exercise his influence beyond his own village.

Religious Influence

The Melanesian big man's functions within the religious system of his society complete the total picture of his influence. In so far as he is able to demonstrate that he possesses *mana*, a special type of spiritual knowledge and supernatural power, he commands respect.

No discussion of Melanesian culture can be considered complete without touching upon the concept of *mana*. Codrington (1891) first brought this concept to the attention of the anthropological world. *Mana*, to the Melanesian, is an invisible power believed to cause all such effects as transcend the people's conception of the normal course of nature. It resides in spiritual beings, either in the spiritual part of living men or in the ghosts of the dead. This power is given by invoking the names of the spirits or ghosts, or by the living or lifeless things to which this mysterious influence is attached. Through *mana* men control or direct the forces of nature, cause sickness or remove it, know the future, and bring prosperity or curse. One is said either to have *mana*, or that *mana* can be with him. Belief in this supernatural power is the foundation of the rites and practices called religion. All magic and witchcraft draw their origins from *mana*.

The big man possesses *mana*-like qualities in his control over the supernatural. In effect, the supernatural sanctions him and supports his authority as a big man. He shows specific strengths in various aspects of the supernatural, whether sickness, control of the weather, witchcraft, dreams, prophecy and divination, ordeals, poisons, or curses. In all these, whatever is done is believed to be effected by the *mana* of spirits and ghosts acting through various media and brought about by secret forms of words through which the power to work is given. The big man does not seem to be adversely affected by his control of *mana*. If the power invoked responds in the manner the big man desired, all is well and good. If it does not, the result is simply not weighed or considered—it is unimportant.

The Mengen Big Man

There are two ways of visualizing the big man in Mengen society. One way is to see him as one who creates new traits or patterns, or who, through the weight of his influence, secures popular acceptance for cultural items from outside the village sphere. An example of one having these characteristics is Koki, a Mengen member of the national parliament, or Painap, a member of the provincial assembly. A second way to conceptualize the Mengen big man is as one who influences the society towards conservatism, thus helping maintain traditional cultural traits and patterns. Talusina, the *maga tamana* 'father of the village' of Manginuna Village where the author resides, depicts this latter type.

The *maga tamana* fills a social role in each Mengen village, a role that is perceived to have existed throughout history. It seems apparent that this role pervades the culture and in many ways unites the entire society. For this reason, I consider Talusina as the one who fills this role, rather than either Koki or Painap.

A Mengen Maga Tamana

Talusina has come to our house to visit probably more than any other villager. He wants us to depend on him for many things. For example, he is our main language helper and often corrects our speech. He is sometimes critical of the way others have taught us to speak the Mengen language. Further, if our supply of *kaukau* (a local type of sweet potato) is ever depleted, he has advised us that we should ask him for more. He is the only villager who has said that we could go to his *aibika* plot and take all that we want to eat of this green leafy vegetable. In these ways he certainly fits the picture of generosity of the Melanesian-styled big man.

Talusina often expresses an interest in what we are doing and where we are going. When someone comes to the village to see us, he may come to our house later to discover who was visiting us and what we talked about. Upon first moving into the village, we visited every family, and on many of the first visits we made, he came to the house where we were sitting to find out what we were doing and interjected his help as we tried to speak the local language. This interest in us appears to be part of his overall responsibility of maintaining village harmony.

The prestige that has been ascribed to the *maga tamana* is reflected in many ways. He is a village supervisor, seeing that plans and preparations, e.g., for a village dance festival, run smoothly, even if he or his family are not directly involved. His family does not seem to enjoy any special status in the village. He does not seem to go to the garden as frequently as other men and will do menial tasks in the village such as repairing a grass

roof or mending a fishing net. He does not chew betel nut,[2] but he does
not seem to be averse to it and he even keeps a container of lime for
those in the village who do chew.

Talusina has achieved his place and attendant privileges in the village
by filling the role of *maga tamana* within the society. His primary task is
the creation and intensification of social relations inside Manginuna Village. We have experienced this first hand in his relations with us as
"whiteskins" within the village. He is an individual whom one should not
unduly anger, since, if his personal emotions were to become involved in
a village case, he could not play the part of the judicial arbitrator. In this
role he receives any who have violated a village taboo. They go to him
individually to be cleansed by having words spoken over them and by being ceremonially washed with ginger that he spits over them.

One generation before Talusina, Manginuna Village settled in its present location, and three influential men at that time seem to have led that
settlement. The first letters of their names, U, M, and P, are enshrined
near the village on the billboard that marks the entrance to the U.M.P.
Social Club where villagers gather to drink beer (if there is some on
hand) and socialize. The "P" represents Talusina's father, the *maga
tamana* of Manginuna Village before him. From his father has come
Talusina's general insight into the role, as well as specialized magical
knowledge of the ritual for cleansing those who have broken taboos and
village laws.

People call on Talusina to perform garden magic as they make preparations to plant their fields. He has also performed rites in various locations
of the village, declaring certain areas to be especially inhabited with spirits where people are not allowed to be. In making reference to one of
these areas one day, he stated that as the years have passed there seems
to be less respect toward these places. He did not appear unduly angered
by this, but rather displayed a "that's-the-way-it-goes" attitude. Recently a
work crew came to the village, clearing ground for a new road that will
bypass the village, knocking down many coconut trees in the process.
Talusina's task was then to go to this site alone at night to appease the
spirits in the ground that had become unsettled when the trees fell.

---

2. The fruit of *Areca catecho* (the "areca palm"), chewed along with lime and a type of
   pepper plant throughout Melanesia.

More than ten years ago a type of cargo cult[3] came into the area. One of several features of this new belief includes a daily afternoon walk to the village cemetery to bear cooked food in honor of the ancestors. If they so desire, the people can also carry an offering of money. In every case it is village women who make this daily trek, led by Talusina who, in his role as *maga tamana*, supervises this rite.

Maga Tamana as Unifier of the Society

The *maga tamana* is one of the most important cohesive aspects of the Mengen society. Françoise and Michel Panoff, a French anthropological team working with the Australian National University, spent approximately two years among the Mengen in the late 1960s, publishing a series of articles (see bibliography) about the society. Information from some of these articles seems to confirm the present research regarding the role of *maga tamana* particularly in regard to his unifying function.

The *maga tamana* has important ritual functions in the village life. He is thought to have knowledge regarding which plants can be used to increase the fertility of food crops at various stages of their development. In severe medical cases he, as a "specialist," often prepares the medication which may either be an herbal one or a Western pharmaceutical product and administers it to the patient. For minor ailments any relative or friend can treat a patient.

Another main function, in addition to overall village harmony, is to make the village prosperous and provide good crops. If he is displeased with other villagers, he may use magic to prevent good crops and village prosperity. When his anger has been appeased, he can call the "soul" of the garden crop back into the garden.

As *maga tamana*, Talusina's father was the most prominent man among the founders of the village. "Father of the village" was seen as his "office." He set up the *sasavanga* 'sacred area' and then took charge of the religious rites which it entailed. Through adequate rites, the function of the *sasavanga* was to ensure prosperity, especially in helping plants to

---

3. This is called by some a type of "money cult." It began in the late 1960s, perhaps by Koriam Urekit, then Member for National Parliament for this area. Some of its characteristics follow. There are posts in each village with roman numerals I to X on them, representing the Ten Commandments, the "code of ethics" for the good life. Each family unit is encouraged to have a small house near theirs as a type of "ancestor" house. There is also a large house in each cemetery where daily gifts of cooked food or money are brought. Over the years this money has been deposited in a bank account from which the people have helped finance many worthwhile community and building projects. The chewing of betel nut is also discouraged among its adherents. An increasing number of people, especially the younger generation, have become disenchanted with its beliefs.

grow and pigs to multiply. The *maga tamana* is responsible for the welfare of the community. He is the primary one to grant permission to any others who want to live in their village (although in our case we dealt only with the village's recognized governmental liaison).

Succession to the office of *maga tamana* is open to both his matrilineal and patrilineal male descendents, provided he was born in, and continues to live in, the hamlet concerned. (See the following section regarding Talusina's first-born as his successor.)

The Mengen and Melanesian "Big Men" Compared

The *maga tamana* represents a "big man" in the Mengen way of thinking. However, comparing and contrasting the typical Melanesian big man with the counterpart reveals more differences than similarities between the two. Let us now consider them in regard to their qualifications and their influences in the economic, sociopolitical, and religious spheres of the society. Figure 1 presents a summary of this discussion.

Qualifications

Talusina has attempted to develop a situation of loyalty between himself and us with an increasing dependence of one upon the other. This is clearly a trait of the aspiring big man.

There is no general tendency among the Mengen for any individual to amass a greater amount of wealth than any other. The Panoffs may have hit upon one of the constraints that has been imposed on the Mengen society to discourage the accumulation of wealth. They refer to a strong "magico-political" movement which calls on the authority of the Ten Commandments (F. Panoff 1969, 1970 and M. Panoff 1970; see also footnote 3). Through this any follower is subject to a leveling policy of "brotherhood." Care must be taken when someone ventures to advance himself economically, as this could lead to a "breach of discipline".

A Mengen associate discussed this constraint of self-advancement from the insider's view. According to the matrilineal rules of Mengen society this man received land through his mother, but this land is located nearer to another village than his own. He personally has planted approximately 600 young coconut trees on this land, and feels that the people of his village are really quite lazy in some respects, i.e., in not developing their own land to any extent. In actual fact, it may be that he desires to advance himself economically, while his fellow villagers want to subject themselves to the leveling policy of "brotherhood."

	Big Man	Maga Tamana
Develops personal loyalty	+	+
Accumulates wealth	+	−
Can pass position on to descendents	−	+
Most often the clan leader	+	−
Prestige ascribed to the role	−	+
Prestige achieved by the person	+	−
Instrument of social control	+	+
Carries special insignias of rank	+	−
Has renown; praised by his fellows	+	−
Exercises influence beyond home village	+	−
Importance transcends various clans	−	+
Controls activities or domains valued by others	+	+
"Plays down" his importance in the village	+	+
Possesses *mana*-like powers	+	+

Figure 1. Comparison of *maga tamana* and Melanesian "big man"

Furthermore Talusina's brother was once employed by the local provincial high school as their trade store proprietor. As the story goes, the Board of Governors of the high school, primarily fellow Mengen, wanted the brother replaced as proprietor since his house and goods were seen to be a bit better than others of the community. They thought he might have been "feathering his own nest." On the one hand, Mengen can leave their village area, get formal education, and aspire to positions outside the village with a cash income, but on the other hand, the individual is discouraged from showing signs of wealth in his home setting.

The *maga tamana* generally thinks first of passing on his role, with its accompanying rights and privileges, to one of his sons, preferably the first-born. But with Talusina, his own sons may not automatically aspire to such a position because of social change. For example, his oldest son is working in a finance office in Rabaul, the provincial capital of New Britain. Although he is thinking of marrying a Mengen girl, it is generally felt that he has removed himself too far from the culture to become his father's replacement.

The *maga tamana* is not necessarily the clan leader, i.e., the oldest male in the clan, as is frequently the case with the Melanesian big man.

Koki and Painap, as more representative of big men, show a greater tendency to achieve prestige than does the *maga tamana*. They have entered national and provincial government positions, respectively. There is some uncertainty as to what degree cargo thinking was a factor in their getting elected. Part of Koki's campaign for the national parliament included posters claiming he was "running in the spirit of Koriam" (see footnote 3). His local political party, the Kivung, also encouraged Painap to compete for the provincial seat. In each case, both men have qualities much admired by the Mengen. Whereas Koki is a short, rather plump man (a feature somewhat admired) and a congenial hand-shaker, Painap is seen as a calm person, not easily angered, and concerned about the needs of the Mengen.

Sociopolitical Influence

As a vital factor in the functioning of his society, the Melanesian big man may carry special insignias of his rank. As a point of observation, Talusina is the only one I have noticed, among all the villagers, carrying a rosary with him to the Catholic worship services.

Both the big man and the *maga tamana* function as instruments of social control in the domains and actions of the people. It will be interesting to see if the *maga tamana* continues to maintain his specific role within the cargo or money cult and among those Mengen who have lately begun to cast aside the tenets of that cult.

For the Melanesian big man, having high rank means having renown and being praised, even directly to his face. But this is not done toward Talusina. Further, the big man is often treated with exceptional politeness and bountiful hospitality outside his village, but the *maga tamana* is unknown by name in any village other than his own. Both Koki and Painap are the ones who, due to their outside political activities, exercise considerable influence in affairs beyond their own villages in the style of the true "big man" and are generally treated with politeness and respect when visiting other villages.

Talusina is the leader of village politics in the traditional sense, but this contrasts with the typical Melanesian big man. The big man is often considered "big" primarily in the eyes of his clan mates, but Talusina's role places him over the entire village comprised of a number of clans, making him an even greater unifying force.

Religious Influence

The influence of the *maga tamana* is perhaps seen more readily within the religious system, the sphere in which Talusina most prominently affects the society. But like the big man, he will have a tendency to play down any major role he might take in the religious sphere. (See also page 5ff.)

If a big man can control some activity, good, or domain which another person values, then he has power over him and can influence his behavior. The *maga tamana* is no doubt recognized as the village leader possessing the most *mana*. Others, however, might show that they also possess *mana* in their roles as healer, sorcerer, or magical practitioner. An example of others is in Manginuna Village who have manifested that they possess *mana* is Magalkena, whom we have seen go out onto the reef in the face of a threatening rainstorm and drive it away. Or Lalumanrea, who, with his ten or so dogs, will call on the spirits before heading into the bush and, if everything is in order, never fail to bring back a wild pig. Talusina, however, is the one who has the special power to pronounce a taboo or a curse on some thing, action, or place.

Conclusion

Based on research and village experience, the present study compares and contrasts the typical big man in Melanesian society with the *maga tamana* of the Mengen society. Generalizations regarding the big man may not be applied in the same degree in each separate Melanesian society. However, he most generally strives for his role through accumulation of wealth and a creation of obligations toward himself in the debtor/creditor relationship. He is an instrument of social control by demonstrating that he can command respect.

The big man in Mengen society is the one who most adequately possesses influences for conservatism, helping to maintain traditional cultural traits and patterns. These responsibilities are also found in the role of *maga tamana* 'father of the village'. While such similarities exist in some areas, especially in religious influence, the Mengen big man actually differs in many more ways from the typical Melanesian big man. The father of the village is a man of importance and possibly the most significant person within his society. His role includes that of village medical specialist. He further ensures village prosperity, good crops, and the general economic, sociopolitical, and religious welfare of the community.

References

Burns, Tom, Matthew Cooper, and Bradford Wild. 1972. "Melanesian Big Men and the Accumulation of Power." *Oceania* 43:104–12.

Chowning, Ann. 1977. *An Introduction to the Peoples and Cultures of Melanesia.* Menlo Park: Cummings.

Codrington, Robert H. 1891. *The Melanesians: Studies in their Anthropology and Folk-lore.* New Haven: HRAF Press. (reprinted 1957)

Finney, Ben R. 1968. "Bigfellow Man Belong Business in New Guinea." *Ethnology* 7:394–410. Repub (1971) in *Melanesian Readings on a Culture Area,* ed. by Lewis L. Langness and John C. Weschler Scranton PA: Chandler, pp. 315–32.

Mayers, Marvin K. 1974. *Christianity Confronts Culture.* Grand Rapids: Zondervan.

Oliver, Douglas L. 1955. *A Solomon Island Society.* Cambridge: Harvard University Press.

Panoff, Françoise. 1970. "Maenge Remedies and Conception of Disease." *Ethnology* 9:68–84.

Panoff, Michel. 1970. "Land Tenure Among the Maenge of New Britain." *Oceania* 40:177–94.

Read, Kenneth E. 1946. "Social Organization in the Markham Valley, New Guinea." *Oceania* 17:93–118.

Sahlins, Marshall D. 1963. "Poor Man, Rich Man, Big-man, Chief: Political Types in Melanesia and Polynesia." In *Cultures of the Pacific,* ed. by Thomas G. Harding and Ben J. Wallace, eds. 1970. New York: The Free Press, pp. 203–15.

Salisbury, Richard F. 1964. "Despotism and Australian Administration in the New Guinea Highlands." In *New Guinea: The Central Highlands,* ed. by James B. Watson. (Special Publication of *American Anthropologist* 66.4) pp. 225–39.

"Pigs Are Our Hearts"
A Functional Study of the Pig in Melanesia

Craig Throop

Introduction

Early descriptions of Melanesian societies gave due recognition to the pig as an important element in the culture. It was not until the middle of the twentieth century, however, that anthropologists began to explore the deeper meaning of Melanesian cultural forms in general, and the pig in particular.

The pig is one of the most obvious features of Melanesian societies. Wherever man is found in Melanesia, there the pig can be found also. The tremendous value which is attached to the pig is reflected in the amount of care and attention given to it. For example, the *Encyclopedia of Papua and New Guinea* states that among the Siuai people of southern Bougainville "young pigs are cared for as if they were pets; their food is cooked in one pot with their owners' food; the women premasticate tubers for sickly piglets; and the animals are ritually named, 'baptized', and given magical treatment for ailments" (Ryan 1972:906). The value of pigs to Melanesians is perhaps well summed up in the saying of the Enga people, "Pigs are our hearts."

In Kaulong[1] society also, pigs are very important. Most men and women own at least one pig, and a big man may own four or five. The

---

1. The Kaulong live in southwest New Britain, inland from the government station at Kandrian. They are linguistically and culturally distinct from the coastal peoples although a great deal of borrowing has occurred. The latest available census figures put the population at around 4,000. Contact with the outside came relatively late, around the 1920s and early '30s, and the rate of development has been slower than in most other areas. This has allowed change to occur at a slower rate and has minimized the disruptiveness of outside influences. The Kaulong are chosen for special reference here because they are the group with which the author has had the most contact.

number of pigs is not as important as their size and the formation of their highly valued tusks. Since there are not as many pigs as in the highlands area, caring for them is not as time-consuming because they are able to sustain themselves by foraging in the bush. Pigs may be fed by their own- ers infrequently, and usually only leftover scraps are given to them. Young piglets are leashed to keep them from running away into the bush and becoming feral.

In the following paragraphs I compare and contrast the functions of the pig in traditional Melanesian societies. By looking at the pig in its roles in the economic, social, and religious arenas of Melanesian cultures, it is evi- dent that the pig plays an indispensable part in the maintenance of these societies.

Economic Functions

The economic functions of the pig include that of being a provision for food and an item of exchange.

Food

One of the functions of the pig in Melanesian societies is to provide food. Even in areas that do not depend as much on the pig for food, such as coastal areas where animal protein is available from the sea, the pig still serves as a source of food during certain times of the year (Todd 1934:194).

To date there has been no precise analysis as to exactly how much Melanesians depend on the pig as a regular source for food. Some assert that it contributes very little nutritional value overall (Chowning 1977:27), while others contend that pigs have a tremendous subsistence importance within Melanesia (Vayda et al. 1961). Vayda cites three reasons for his position: pigs are eaten more frequently than has been supposed; they contribute food reserves on the hoof; and their ceremonial function is linked to their subsistence functions in some situations.

Several things must be considered when seeing the pig as a source of food. First, there is considerable variation throughout Melanesia in the use of pigs for food, largely due to the result of different ecological set- tings. Second, many answers have been given on the basis of subjective, impressionistic data, rather than agreed-upon criteria. Therefore, at least a part of the problem might be semantic. Third, it must be determined whether the question is being answered from the viewpoint of the insider or the outsider, both regarding the individual cultures and Melanesia as a whole. Fourth, there is an overlapping of functions of the pig, so that one function may sometimes be camouflaged by another. This underscores a general anthropological principle that in organic societies, to use Durkheim's terminology, functions tend to converge on common forms. Fifth, the dysfunctional, or negative, aspect of the pig must be considered in any overall evaluation, i.e., the pig as a competitor for, and a destructive consumer of, food. Sixth, a distinction may be made between the pig as food to satisfy hunger, and the pig as food to satisfy taste. Seventh, the relative importance of the function of the pig as food will not necessarily be determined by statistics concerning the amount of pork consumed by any particular group on a regular basis since, as Vayda says, pigs may be considered "food reserves on the hoof" in Melanesian societies. Were this not the case, it might be expected that pigs would be eaten more often than they are. To a Melanesian, caught up in the continual quest for food, pigs might be considered "repositories for surplus vegetal produce that might otherwise be unavailable for consumption by people" (Vayda et al. 1961:71).

In some ways the function of the pig as food is bound up with all other functions. This is a recognition of its importance in Melanesian society and suggests that in some way it colors all the other functions. Pigs are not merely food but are a particularly valued kind of food (i.e., meat), and, more than that, they are considered an especially delectable kind of meat.

Exchange

Another economic function of the pig in Melanesia is that of exchange. This may be seen as a function derived from its more basic function as food.

The exchange of pigs for other items of value occurs primarily between groups. Among the islanders of the Vitiaz Strait, pigs may be exchanged for such things as dogs, wooden bowls, pots, canoes, or cash (Harding 1967:35). In some areas of Melanesia various conditions do not encourage trade, but it is felt that even in those areas, should intergroup trading begin, the pig would assume the role of an item of exchange.

Pigs also serve as an exchange item for sociopolitical purposes. They may be used in the bride price or to enhance one's influence or prestige. Among the Kaulong, pigs are also important as items of exchange. They are used as part of the bride price, repayment of a debt, and as trade items both within and outside the community.

Social Functions

The social functions of the pig in Melanesian cultures fall into at least three categories: ceremonial food, a symbol of good relations, and a symbol of wealth, prestige, and power.

Ceremonial

The pig is used extensively in various kinds of ceremonies and celebrations. Rappaport's statement concerning this functional aspect of the pig in Tsembaga serves as a good general statement for Melanesia as a whole: "Tsembaga ritual, . . . like the ritual of many other people in Melanesia, is closely bound up with pigs. Most ritual occasions are marked by the slaughter of pigs and the consumption of pork" (1967:56–57).

The role of the pig in rituals varies according to the purpose of the ritual. In some rituals it is an integral part of the event. There is a particular category of singsings in which the pig is on public display during the celebration. The Kaulong, for example, carry the pig to the location of the singsing and suspend it between two sticks in full view of all the participants. The pig seems to have a subconscious, symbolic significance in this instance, representing man-over-nature, which culminates in the killing of the pig at the close of the event. On other occasions, however, the pig is peripheral to the main event and appears toward the end of the ceremony only as food.

It may be good at this point to discover that which distinguishes the economic function of the pig as food from its social, i.e., ceremonial, function, since in both cases the pig is eaten. Some have suggested that the ceremonial function is simply a derived one, since "the wide distribution of the meat, which rests on the ideal of mutual giving and receiving, makes possible the immediate use of all the food, which would otherwise quickly spoil and be wasted. The grander distributions of pork that occur at the pig-slaughtering ceremonies serve the same function" (Vayda et al. 1961:70). It would be overly simplistic and inaccurate, however, to see the primary function of these celebrations as compensation for the lack of methods for meat preservation in Melanesian culture. While it may be a latent or even a manifest function of the rituals, it is most likely a secondary function. It should be pointed out, too, that in the highlands, pig feasts are often characterized by a prodigal use of pork. The meat is eaten in excessive quantities, and vomiting is sometimes induced so that the person can refill his stomach.

Relational

A second social function of the pig is that of initiating, sustaining, or restoring good interpersonal relations. To give a person a piece of pork is a very significant act and a way of saying that the relationship between the two people is, or must return to, a friendly, congenial one. Among the Kaulong, also, the pig is used for this purpose. The distribution of pork on any given ceremonial occasion is a good index of culturally significant relationships. An important social relationship is between affinal kin. Thus a man's affines will often receive the choicest portions of pork.

The distribution of pork seems to follow certain general patterns which vary in specific details from culture to culture. Concerning the Tsembaga people, Rappaport states that ". . . pigs killed in the context of misfortune or emergency apparently tend to be consumed by those who are either victims of or participants in the event, or by those close to them . . . there is a tendency to distribute widely the meat that results from the killing of pigs for reasons other than misfortune or emergency" (1967:84). Ceremonial exchanges of pigs are especially important in the highlands for cementing relations between families or clans or for restoring peaceful relations between warring groups.

Symbolic

Another social function of pigs is as a symbol of wealth, prestige, and power. In this way they tie in closely with the "big man" system. Among the Siuai "pig ownership is considered essential for adult socio-economic status. To shout at a person, 'you have no pigs', is to offer him an insult" (Oliver 1955:348). Chowning points out that one of the essential qualities of a big man is success in the accumulation of wealth, and she puts pigs as the primary source of wealth (1977:42). Among the Kaulong, a big man without pigs would be a contradiction in terms. Part of the definition of a big man is that he has several pigs, or that he owns a large tusker, or that at any given time he has the potential for assembling a significant number of pigs through repayment obligations.

Pigs are a form of capital to a big man. He can use them to repay a debt or to make compensation. He may also put someone in his debt by giving him a pig or by giving away substantial portions of pork at a feast. Reciprocation may take place in both instances, but if it does not, a genuine big man will usually not insist on repayment, preferring instead the increase in prestige and influence that results.

When a big man's kin are involved, however, interaction with them has an element of social responsibility and expectation which interaction with nonkin does not have. Thus, if a big man gives a pig to one of his kin and is not reciprocated (which is unlikely anywhere), there is not necessarily any increase in the big man's prestige in the eyes of the community.

Another aspect of this function of the pig is that in many Melanesian societies carved pig tusks are among the most prized of possessions. The Kaulong consider them very valuable as they greatly enhance a person's prestige. Great care is exercised in raising pigs with these large tusks. One of the most sought-after items in the trading system described by Harding is the boar's tusk. As he points out, the value of these tusks is determined by their size and the extent of their curvature so that "those tusks that have grown to the point where the 'eye' of the tooth nearly meets the base, thus forming a circle, are considered to be the most valuable" (Harding 1967:47–48).

Religious Functions

In addition to the economic and social functions of the pig are what might be termed its religious functions, including the pig as a source of vital strength and as a sacrifice. These are religious functions because they relate to supernatural beliefs and practices and carry the widespread Melanesian belief that pigs have souls. However, as Codrington pointed out when speaking of the Florida people in the Solomon Islands, the soul of a pig is not thought of as being the same as that of the soul of man, since as his informant put it, "When a man dies his *tarunga* ['soul'] is a *tindalo*, a ghost, and who ever heard of a pig *tindalo*?" (Codrington 1957:249).

The reply of Codrington's informant shows that he distinguishes between the soul of man and the soul of a pig on the basis of its ability to survive beyond death. There could be other things which figure in the distinction, but the informant probably responded on the basis of what to him was the most characteristic distinction between the two. Nevertheless, it seems likely that the vitalizing force of the pig plays an important part in the two religious functions of vital strength and sacrifice.

Vital Strength

The pig as a source of vital strength to the eater is a subset of a larger set of beliefs prevalent among Melanesians, namely, that various kinds of soul powers and strengths are to be derived from the nature of whatever object is eaten.[2] The Kaulong specifically believe that by eating certain parts of a pig a person gains the special qualities and particular powers associated with those parts. These are over and above the physical strength which results from eating the meat.

Sacrifice

Another religious function of the pig is the sacrificial function. In Melanesian societies the pig is used to appease the ancestors or spirits in some way. Gitlow says that among the Mt. Hagen tribes ". . . the vital attribute of the pig, which gives it great value in the native's eyes, is religious rather than economic. . . . the pig is the only means by which the native is able to influence the spirits in his behalf" (1947:56). It would appear, however, that this function of the pig is primarily confined to highland groups.

According to one recent comparative study, there is an "incest taboo" in the lowlands against killing and eating one's own pigs. This is correlated to lack of incidences of specific sacrifices to spirits. In the highlands, however, no such taboo exists and pigs are sacrificed to ancestor and other spirits and are consumed by one's own groups and one's associates (Rubel and Rosman 1978:312). The authors of the study also point out the appropriateness of the pig as a sacrifice in highlands societies:

> Pigs sacrificed to spirits serve a twofold purpose, exchanges with men and exchanges with spirits. None of the other objects exchanged in these societies has this twofold capacity, that is, alive and given to spirits, killed and cooked and given to men (p. 312).

It has been difficult to detect direct evidence which would point to the existence of a sacrificial function of the pig in Kaulong culture. Part of the problem in questioning individuals is that they are often hesitant to reveal beliefs and practices which are disapproved of by the mission in the area. However, it has been observed that burial rites always involve the killing of a pig or pigs. According to George Brown (1910), in northeast New Britain the killing of pigs at funerals is definitely associated with the soul of the departed individual. If his analysis is valid, it is possible that the belief might also be found among other New Britain people.

---

2. This belief seems to underlie some forms of cannibalism in the past in which it was believed that by eating various parts of the corpse the soul powers connected with those parts would become a part of the person eating them. This is also seen in the eating of various types of birds and animals. So it is not surprising, then, to find it in connection with the pig.

Conclusion

A look at the function of the pig in Melanesia has confirmed its importance as a cohesive element in the society. The pig appears to be a focus
on integration of all aspects of the culture and a valuable point of reference in describing some of the deeper processes at work within those cultures. This paper has touched upon many of the important values of the
pig in Melanesian culture. These have included its use as food; its essential role in ceremonial, interpersonal, and symbolic social relationships;
and its importance as a sacrifice and as a source of vital strength. This
study has underscored the usefulness of functional descriptions in anthropological studies by going beyond a purely ethnographic description and
looking at the pig as an integrating force and a pervasive cultural theme.

Though the pig is vital to Melanesian culture, gaps have been found in
the literature that reveal a need for further research concerning its role in
the society. For a fuller treatment of the pig in Melanesia, the following
topics should be dealt with: (1) to draw together into a typological format
the different functions of the pig as they are found within various Melanesian cultures; (2) to correlate the value of the pig as food with its value as
an item of exchange, in order to determine whether this correlation is
modified by factors such as the principle of supply and demand; and (3)
to investigate more intensively the function of the pig as a sacrifice in
lowland cultures.

References

Brown, George. 1910. *Melanesians and Polynesians*. London: Macmillan.

Chowning, Ann. 1973. "Child Rearing and Socialization." In *Anthropology
in Papua New Guinea,* ed. by Ian Hogbin. Melbourne: Melbourne
University Press, pp. 61–79.

————. 1977. *An Introduction to the Peoples and Cultures of Melanesia*.
Menlo Park, CA: Cummings.

Codrington, Robert H. 1957. *The Melanesians: Studies in their Anthropology and Folk-lore*. New Haven: HRAF Press. (edition of 1891 re-
published)

Gitlow, Abraham L. 1947. *Economics of the Mount Hagen Tribes, New Guinea*. (American Ethnological Society, monograph 12) Seattle: Univ. of Washington Press.

Harding, Thomas G. 1967. *Voyagers of the Vitiaz Strait: A Study of a New Guinea Trade System*. Seattle: Univ. of Washington Press.

Oliver, Douglas L. 1955. *A Solomon Islands Society: Kinship and Leadership among the Siuai of Bougainville*. Cambridge: Harvard Univ. Press.

Rappaport, Roy A. 1967. *Pigs for the Ancestors: Ritual in the Ecology of a New Guinea People*. New Haven: Yale Univ. Press.

Ryan, Peter, ed. 1972. *Encyclopedia of Papua and New Guinea*. Melbourne: Melbourne University Press. 3 vols.

Rubel, Paula G. and Abraham Rosman. 1978. *Your Own Pigs You May Not Eat*. Chicago: University of Chicago Press.

Strathern, Andrew 1971. "Pig Complex and Cattle Complex: Some Comparisons and Counterpoints." *Man* 8:2.

Todd, J.A. 1934–35. "Report on Research Work in Southwest New Britain, Territory of New Guinea." *Oceania,* 5:80–101, 193–213.

Vayda, Andrew P., A. Leeds, and D.B. Smith. 1961. "The Place of Pigs in Melanesian Subsistence." In *Symposium: Patterns of Land Utilization and other Papers*. (Proceedings of the 1961 annual spring meeting of the American Ethnological Society. ed. by Viola E. Garfield) Seattle: American Ethnological Society. pp. 69–77.

Of Pigs, Men, and Life:
A Glimpse at Wiru Society

Michael Fullingim

Introduction

One of the first entries in my Wiru-English dictionary[1] was the word *kai*, along with its English gloss 'pig'. Because the Wiru exhibit such an inveterate interest in their pigs, just as all other major highlands cultures do in Papua New Guinea (PNG), I have recently concluded that if *kai* is to be properly defined, it must be defined socially.

Background

My intention in this paper is to provide this enhanced social definition for "*kai*—n., pig". My operating assumptions for a social theory are derived from the classic "Structure-Functionalism" of A.R. Radcliffe-Brown. In order to explicate his notion of structure-function as it relates to society, Radcliffe-Brown utilizes the metaphor of an animal organism. He agreed with Durkheim that ". . . the 'function' of a social institution is the correspondence between it and the needs . . . of the social organism [society] . . . ." (1952:178). However, Radcliffe-Brown felt that it was necessary to refine this definition by further asserting that ". . . the organism is *not* itself the structure; it is a collection of units . . . arranged in a structure; i.e. in a set of relations; the organism (society) *has* a structure" (p. 179). Therefore, if the structure is the set of relations between entities, it follows that the structural continuity of the organism is maintained by a

---

1. During the period from October 1975 to April 1979 my wife and I and two children worked under the auspices of the Wesleyan Church Corporation as missionary linguists and field anthropologists among the Wiru, a group of approximately 19,000 who live in the southeastern portion of the Southern Highlands Province of Papua New Guinea. Compilation of a Wiru-English dictionary was a natural by-product of our major task—translation of the New Testament into Wiru.

"life-process," which "consists of the activities and interactions of the con-
sistent units of the organism" (p. 179). Hence, the life of an organism
(i.e., society) is considered to be "the *functioning* of its structure." And
now, the metaphor is complete:

(cell : organ :: individual : institution)

Be it cell, organ, individual or institution, each "has an *activity* and that
activity has a *function*" within the total structure.

However, if the study at hand is to stand on yet a firmer structure-functionalist foundation, then the further notion of "functional unity" must be
assumed as a primitive. The social life of a community, as defined by
Radcliffe-Brown, is the *functioning* of its social structure. Moreover, the
function of any recurrent activity ". . . is the *part* it plays in the social life
as a *whole* and therefore the contribution it makes to the maintenance of
the structural continuity" (p. 180, emphasis mine). Thus, one major tenet
of the structure-functionalist social theory is that

> a social system (the total social structure of a society together with the
> totality of social usages in which the structure appears and on which it de-
> pends for its continued existence) has a certain kind of unity, which we may
> speak of as a functional unity (p. 181).

It is precisely this notion of functional unity that permits the analyst to focus on a "part"—a partial activity—and to investigate the set of relations
among the parts, or the unit entities, and thereby gain access to the
"whole" of the social structure and, at the same time, hold in tension the
truth of the axiom, that "the whole is greater than the sum of its parts."

Hypotheses

Applying these theoretical considerations to the present study, I have
formulated the following hypothesis as a research heuristic:

> (P-1) Given the pig is a partial entity with Wiru society, if the set of rela-
> tions enmeshing this entity, the pig, provide an access to, serve to explain,
> or even construct a sizeable portion of the whole social structure, then the
> functional relationship of the pig is to be considered as a central, primary
> contribution to the maintenance of the structural continuity of the whole
> (i.e., Wiru social life in its totality).

The remainder of the paper presents my analysis of the perceived set
of relations involving the pig. A second order, working-level hypothesis
proposes the analytical usefulness of conceptually viewing these commonly
accepted relationships as either of two types:

> (P-2) Any given activity involving a pig will necessarily relate to the *pig-as-
> animal* or to the *pig-as-symbol*.

Participant observation and personal field notes have provided the primary source of data, and current anthropological literature on related highland groups of PNG has been drawn upon secondarily.

The Pig—Both Animal and Symbol

Whenever I go to a state fair in my home country and see registered Hampshire pigs or Santa Gertrudes beef cattle, I see primarily this: livestock being raised for human consumption and economic gain—nothing more and nothing less. Wearing such "spectacles" as this in a highlands society of PNG will assuredly lead an observer to a host of erroneous assumptions regarding the relationship of pig husbandry to the total social structure.

Pigs are of great interest to the Wiru, but they are not such an exclusive concern as are the herds of pastoralists. Evans-Pritchard described the relationship between the Nuer and their cattle in terms of an intimate symbiotic relationship in which "cattle and men sustain life by their reciprocal services to one another" (1940:36f), thus forming a single community of the closest kind. Although this kind of intimate relationship is not evident between the Wiru and their pigs, on the other hand, no competent observer would imagine that their purpose of keeping pigs is simply dietary. It is not possible to account for the expansive demand for pigs throughout Wiru social life on alimentary grounds alone. This is the first hint for conceptually setting up a dichotomy to facilitate examining the network of relationships in which the pig plays a vital role.

Pig-as-animal indicates those activities and relationships within an individual family unit issuing from the task of pig husbandry per se. Questions that have guided my investigation for this phase have been of the following nature. Who owns pigs? How are pigs raised and cared for? Where are pigs raised? Who is responsible for the various aspects of domestication?

Pig-as-symbol indicates those activities and relationships extending beyond the family or clan and issuing from ceremonial exchange. Questions for explicating this second phase have been of the following type: What are pigs used for? When are pigs utilized in the various ways? Who is responsible for exchanging pigs? And there was always that elusive question regarding motivation—Why all the "fuss"?

The two parts of this dichotomy (i.e., pig-as-animal and pig-as-symbol) relate to each other temporally as well as pragmatically. For example, a small piglet must be nurtured and domesticated for one to two years *before* it acquires the status of pig-as-symbol (a temporal consideration).

Once a pig has entered the pig-as-symbol network, it nevertheless must still be cared for and maintained (a pragmatic consideration). Hence, pig-as-animal and pig-as-symbol are not polar opposites, but rather one overlays the other, and they both remain distinct in function. Pig-as-animal spells "hard work," whereas pig-as-symbol spells "prestige." The simple diagram below (fig. 1) attempts to illustrate the relationship between these terms.

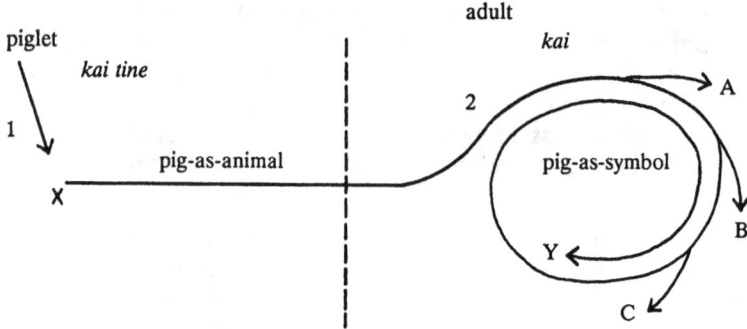

Figure 1. Twofold conceptualization of the pig

Figure 1 as a whole represents the pig herd of a typical Wiru family. The time-line x——y represents the perpetual aspect of pig-as-animal; for as long as the family has pigs, it must work to feed and maintain them. Numbers 1 and 2 indicate the two major sources for increasing the size of the pig herd: piglets acquired through birth or wild piglets captured and adult pigs acquired through ceremonial exchanges. The spiraling circle represents the pig-as-symbol network. The letters A, B, and C, represent occasions of reduction in the size of the pig herd; hence, the graphic centrifugal "spin offs" illustrate the fact that the family is no longer responsible for the care of pigs that are ceremonially given away.

Pig-as-animal

Ethnographies of various tribes throughout the Central Highlands of PNG are replete with accounts of the different aspects of pig husbandry.[2] Rappaport (1968), for instance, presents a detailed study of Maring pig husbandry and, in part, attempts to technically measure some of the "costs" of intensified husbandry, particularly those of providing fodder and times when pigs are ceremonially given away. Watson (1977)

---

2. See also Strathern 1971 and Meggitt 1971 for husbandry practices among the Melpa and the Mae Enga, respectively. See Rubel and Rosman 1978, as well as Brown 1978 for general comparative accounts.

describes the "Jones Effect" (i.e., in places where pigs are mutually exchanged, the expansion of pig production in some part of a network leads to expanding production in other parts), and he argues that this principle, better than others proposed thus far, accounts for recent ecological developments in the Central Highlands region and how they have rapidly spread through the area.

Coupled with the insights on particulars that I have gleaned from these various accounts and arguments, I have been prompted to conclude that the Wiru are not ethnic isolates, and consequently their techniques and practices of pig husbandry that I have described below are but paraphrases (or in structuralist terms, transformations; Lévi Strauss 1966:75) of those of other groups in the Highlands. But of course ethnographers have long noticed this feature of cultural commonality for this region of PNG; for example, Glasse and Meggitt (1969:2) assert,

> The technologies and inventories of material culture of these groups (Central Highlanders) are noticeably constant throughout each region. Everywhere pigs are prized, together with other culturally defined valuables, such as shells and plumes.

So it comes as no surprise that every Wiru family owns pigs, and much of their energy and skill is devoted to pig husbandry, though they rarely slaughter swine outside of ritual and ceremonial occasions. Indeed, the Wiru raise pigs to be a member of the family: often sleeping next to them, talking to them, stroking and fondling them, calling them by name, feeding them with choice morsels, leading them on a leash to the gardens where their rooting serves as a primitive "cultivator," and weeping when they fall sick or are injured or are slaughtered in a ceremonial pig kill. Harris refers to this phenomenon as "pig love," a state of total community between man and pig. "In the ambience of pig love one cannot truly be human except in the company of pigs" (1978:39). For a Wiru man not to have pigs is to be considered merely a *rabisman* (Melanesian Pidgin for "a worthless person," hence, "rubbish man").

Raising pigs, however, is primarily the responsibility of the Wiru women. Therefore, pig husbandry is a central point of consideration in the matter of division of labor between male and female, husband and wife, even son and daughter. A typical extended family is composed of husband and wife, three to six children, some of whom may be married and have their own children, a possible grandparent, and an average of six pigs, plus or minus two. With these demands upon her, a wife's daily activities very nearly form a closed set: gardening (i.e., clearing off secondary regrowth and preparing mounds for sweet potato vines, planting, and harvesting of tubers and other vegetables), carrying back from the garden string bags laden with tubers for both family consumption and pig fodder, child rearing, pig tending, and preparing meals.

No pigs are ever allowed to run free within the village perimeter, but rather they are led with a short rope tied to one front leg and then tethered to a post driven into the ground beside the family hut. Pigs are turned out into the bush to forage. As Brown has observed,

> Where pigs and people are few, and agriculture is less intensive, the protection of gardens is not a major concern. But in the areas of concentrated settlement, where pigs break through fences and can destroy large sweet potato gardens, they must be contained (1978:47–48).

Thus, the presence of numerous domestic pigs has created the need for fencing. The main pattern has been to build a fence around the garden, thus allowing pigs the freedom to forage in grass and rain forest. Fence building (with the numerous styles and types partially depending on the garden location and availability of bush materials) is primarily a man's task. Thus, when a pig breaks through someone's garden fence, it predictably results in a heated argument between pig owner and garden owner. In some instances when a pig has damaged a garden, the irate garden owner may kill the pig, thus depriving the pig's owner of a valued property and provoking demand for recompense. In each case, though, it is the men who have to negotiate the appropriate compensatory pay for whatever damages were done. Grievances such as this occupy more time and energy of the men than they would really prefer![3]

Even though the pig forage area may be far from the main village settlement, a well-domesticated pig returns to a house (*kaine yapu* 'pig's house') for feeding and sleep. This control of pig movement and feeding is an important element of husbandry, and it also implies differentiation of male and female roles. A husband has the task of constructing the pighouse, and this utilizes great effort and skill, considering the raw materials available for building. A poorly constructed pighouse is greatly disdained. On the other hand, a well-constructed pighouse provides not only a dry shelter from the tropical rains (averaging 200 inches per year), a place to sleep, and a farrowing facility, but most importantly, a familiar place for regular, patterned human-pig interaction. A wife has the primary responsibility of training the pigs, starting the process ideally with piglets. They are fondled and hand-fed daily, even occasionally nursed by the woman who cares for them. By having a rope tied to its front leg, a pig may be led about by its owners, kept in or near houses in different areas, or tethered. The provision of food and shelter certainly binds the pigs to their

---

3. Note how the relations surrounding pig-as-animal can quickly take the investigator into the various forms and functions of fence construction, conceptions of owner responsibility and socially accepted response-behavior regarding the discovered destruction, the traditional legal patterns, as well as the current village court system, particularly in regard to its perceived ability to deal satisfactorily with minor grievances before they become major.

owners, but pigs do often wander off for some time and a few become feral. A poorly trained pig reflects negatively on a wife's pig-tending skills.

Since boars are inclined to ill temper and also have little fat, a boar must be more constrained than a gelding or sow. Hence for these reasons as well as the potential complications resulting from sequential, multi-ownership via ceremonial pig exchanges, nearly all male piglets are castrated. In fact, in the region where I worked there were no domesticated adult boars. Hence, sows interbreed with feral boars, the wild strain is perpetuated, and the result does not produce many large, fat pigs. A lactating sow often becomes very thin. Generally, litters are small, only three to four piglets with few of these surviving; pigs grow slowly and are not fattened quickly for slaughter. Pig-raising is not easy, for pigs become sick, lost, or stolen by hostile neighbors, and this upsets plans for the social-ritual-ceremonial activities involving the pig-as-symbol.

A Wiru family therefore devotes much thought and planning to its pigs. Families manage their domestic herd numbers and sizes by exchange, purchase, loan, donation, fattening, and restraining. They may even have their pigs under the care of relatives in other areas for a time when disease threatens or the household is otherwise strained (since the more adult pigs, the more sweet potato fodder is needed—provided, of course, through intensified gardening efforts). When preparing for a large feast, much of the burden of feeding may be shifted to these relatives, who will later be rewarded with pork. A pig cared for by another may later be killed, cooked, and given to the person as a ceremonial presentation. Or if a sow has a litter, the caretaker may receive one or more of the offspring.

Pig-as-symbol

The foregoing discussion regarding the pig-as-animal, i.e., the pragmatic aspects of pig husbandry, is short-lived and relatively dry reading if it fails to recognize the paramount aspect of pig-as-symbol—the "prestige syndrome" (Watson 1977:61). "Nowhere in New Guinea are pigs a common item of diet; everywhere the killing of a pig is a matter for feast and celebration" (Brown 1978:87). Hence, domestic pigs are part of the household valuable property—their raising, use, and slaughter are equally purposeful. Watson (1977) claims that,

> so keen is the need for pigs for exchange purposes that one can understand why observers long held that these purposes, rather than nourishment, constituted the true importance of pigs in Melanesia (1977:63).

Consequently, the discussion below will delineate the "multi-focality" (Turner 1967:50; 1968:52) of the pig-as-symbol among the Wiru. Figure 2 represents a preliminary conceptualization of the pig-as-symbol as nucle-ating the whole of Wiru social life, and it should be referred to by the reader throughout the discussion in order to maintain perspective in rela-tion to the greater whole.

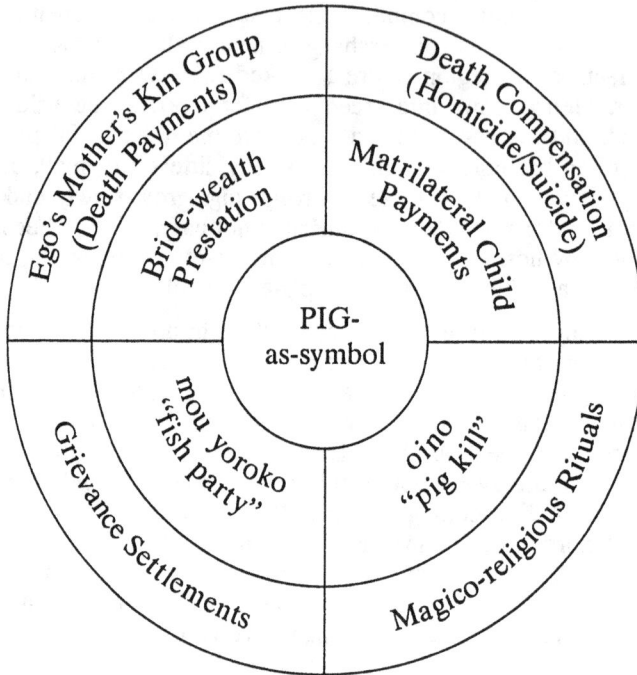

Figure 2. Pig-as-symbol in relation to the whole of Wiru social life

Pig-as-symbol is the phrase that I am using to refer to the set of activi-ties in which pigs are used to extend relationships beyond the extended family or clan. In other words, on the way to becoming a protein supple-ment for Wiru consumers, the pig symbolizes and satisfies other powerful demands of its users. A number of these simply cannot be satisfied with-out the use of pigs, and these are embedded in some of the most critical aspects of Wiru social life. Symbolizing not only wealth and positive social well-being, the pig is also the symbolic form in which reciprocal relation-ships are developed and cemented. In an earlier paper (1980a) I wrote extensively on this feature of *reciprocity* among the Wiru as an all-pervasive system.

In that paper, I explained in detail the different, but nevertheless inter-related, occasions for kinship-centered (affinal) reciprocal gift-giving: bride-wealth presentations and the subsequent *yagi toko* gifts; matrilateral child payments (Strathern 1971a), and the wife's brother-sister's husband dyad; two kinds of death payments to affines, known as *kage wiko* and *kioli toko;* and ceremonial pearlshell giving. I further noted that other types of reciprocal exchanges are, conceptually speaking, socially centered—not that they are different in principle, but rather they are on a different level of the social hierarchy (i.e., not family or clan, not affinal, but allies and/or enemies), and yet these, the most ostentatious of all ceremonies that the Wiru involve themselves in, are part and parcel of the total, complex structure of reciprocal relationships. The three ceremonial occasions referred to are the *mou yoroko* 'fishcooking (ceremony)', the *oino* 'major pig-killing festival', and the unpredicted death compensation presentations (either for homicide, regardless of location of occurrence, or for suicide, when it occurs in a "foreign" place, i.e., in a nonclan territory).

For the purpose of this study the most significant observation regarding all these ceremonies is that pigs are the dominant symbolic forms used to materialize the concerned relationships. The prestige of owning and exchanging pigs unquestionably acts as a powerful synergist. Watson's general cultural statement applies to the Wiru situation down to the details.

> For scarce imports of great value; for brides; for children; for death payments; for establishing, cementing, and maintaining friendships and alliances; for bribes and secret payments to ensorcel or slay; for wergild; for peace-making; for personal prestige-seeking and tokens of status; for medico-magical purposes; for the maintenance or expansion of security —for all of these purposes pigs are precious (1977:63).

It is hardly conceivable in these circumstances that a Wiru family could have too many pigs, except for the cost of maintaining them.

However, that cost must be balanced against the cost of *not* having pigs. And the cost of not having pigs rises appreciably in a social and economic structure where pigs have such multiple and expansible uses as delineated above. Moreover, the cost of not having pigs rises where more exchangers use pigs, or some exchangers begin using more pigs, for goods whose scarcity has not lessened or whose utility has increased. Such scarce goods include women.

The following text is my translation of a portion of an extended discourse by an older Wiru man regarding changes in the bride-wealth presentation, and thereby implies the problem of the cost of not having pigs.

> When I married this woman, this pig bone we call *lapai* ('skull bone') is what I used in order to get married. 'My father' got 'my mothers'; so 'my mothers' along with others now were obtained with pearlshells and those kinds of things. Redman (referring to me, hence, to all European expatriates), you came and now I have to 'buy' a woman! Before, it was not done this way. (They) got 'my mother' with pig's teeth. (They) got 'my mother'

with pig spinal bones. And so (they) got 'my mother' with the pig skull bone *(lapai)*. And so with a cassowary bird egg which is laid, and with this *ponopo* headband which they made, they got a woman.

From a few pig bones, and other seemingly worthless items, the bride-wealth presentation has inflated in less than two generations to thirteen live pigs (@ $300 = $3,900), plus 20 pearlshells (@ $125 = $2,500), plus $400 to $600 in notes, totalling approximately $7,000! This is quite a size-able sum in light of the fact that the average annual per capita income for Papua New Guineans is $350.

At the "fish-cooking" ceremony *(mou yoroko)* that was staged in Alia village on July 15, 1978, the following goods were distributed in ritual cer-emony to eight opposing clans from neighboring villages: 57 pigs (i.e., 228 quarters of pork), 12 quarters of beef, 223 cartons of canned mackerel, and 83 bags of rice each weighing 25 kilograms—totaling approximately $21,640! But this exchange was a minor one when compared with the ones (the *oino* pig-kill) that took place the following month (August 1978) on the other side of the Wiru valley. On one given day six separate vil-lages killed, butchered, cooked and distributed nearly 2,400 pigs (a whop-ping 9,600 quarters of pork) to their allied clans from opposing villages. In contrast to the *mou yoroko* ceremony, only pigs are distributed in the *oino* ceremony, and the value of 2,400 pigs is approximately $720,000.

There is obviously an intimate relationship between prestige and the control of economic resources in Wiru society, a society that accumulates its social surplus labor as capital in the form of pigs in order to be con-verted ultimately into social and political benefits. The strongest incentive for intensive pig husbandry and production of produce (i.e., fodder) would appear to be the desire of Wiru men for prestige and political power.

Conclusion

What motivates a group of people, such as the Wiru, who daily have to scratch out a living in mountainous rain forests, to become involved in such complex patterns of redistribution of enormous amounts of tradition-al wealth (primarily in the form of live pigs and/or pork)? I am not at all confident in suggesting a hypothesis in answer to this question, but it is fairly obvious that the set of relations that functionally involve the pig provides a rather productive access to the total ecological-economic-kin-ship-political-religious structures of the culture. In these structures domes-tic production, interpersonal and intergroup relations, trade, and success are interrelated.

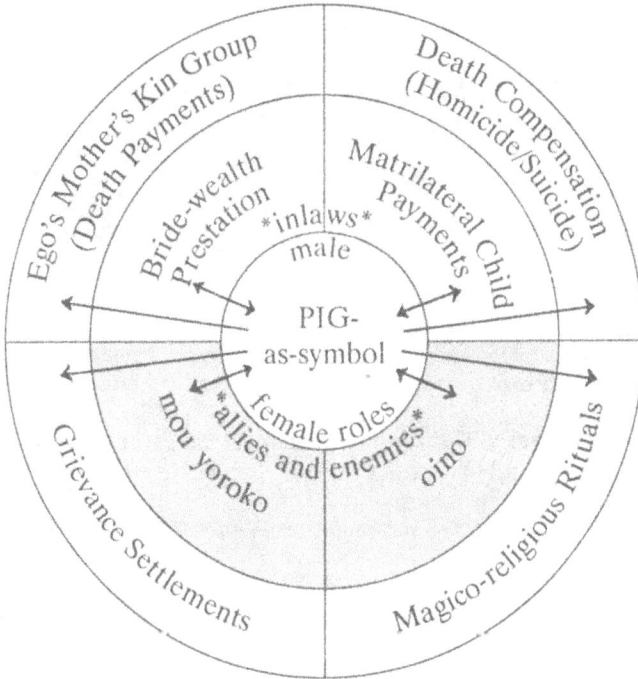

Figure 3. Functional relationship of the pig to the whole of Wiru life

What I have attempted to demonstrate in this study is that when a Wiru uses the word *kai*, he means not only the pig-as-animal but more significantly the pig-as-symbol, a partial cultural entity that nucleates nearly the whole structure of his social life. I have only superficially referred to these multifocal uses of the pig in this paper. The next logical step obviously would be an in-depth analysis of the different social entities (structures) that interface with the pig.

The final diagram, figure 3, is intended to present a refined conceptualization of the pig as a heart-core dynamic of Wiru social life. The double arrow (←→) represents reciprocal exchanges (calculated generosity resulting in staggered debts and repayments); the single arrow (→) represents one-way payments (resulting in permanent reduction of one's pig herd); and the shaded area represents "pork" rather than live pigs. Conversely, the clear areas are those occasions that utilize live pigs only, and this implies that a pig may change owners several times while in the pig-as-symbol network before it comes to the "end" for which every pig is destined.

References

Brown, Paul. 1978. *Highland Peoples of New Guinea*. Cambridge: Cambridge University Press.

Earle, Olive L. 1959. *Pigs, Tame and Wild*. New York: William Morrow.

Evans-Pritchard, E.E. 1940. *The Nuer: A Description of the Modes of Livelihood and Political Institutions of a Nilotic People*. New York: Oxford University Press.

Firth, Raymond. 1973. *Symbol: Public and Private*. Ithaca, N.Y.: Cornell University Press.

Fullingim, J. Michael. 1979. Unpublished field notes on the Wiru, 1975–1979. Southern Highlands Province, Papua New Guinea.

———. 1980a. "Reciprocity Among the Wiru of Papua New Guinea." Unpublished MS.

———. 1980b. "Wiru Folktale Analysis, Papua New Guinea." Unpublished MS.

———. 1980c. "Marxist Anthropological Analysis." Unpublished MS.

Glasse, R.M., and M.J. Meggitt, eds. 1969. *Pigs, Pearlshells, and Women: Marriage in the New Guinea Highlands*. Englewood Cliffs, N.J.: Prentice-Hall.

Harris, Marvin. 1974. *Cows, Pigs, Wars, and Witches: The Riddles of Culture*. New York: Vintage Books.

Kerr, Harland. 1967. "Witu: Essentials for Translation. Anthropology section." Unpublished MS. Summer Institute of Linguistics, Ukarumpa, Papua New Guinea.

———. n.d. "Witu-English Dictionary." Unpublished MS.

Lévi-Strauss, Claude. 1966. *The Savage Mind*. Chicago: University of Chicago Press.

Meggitt, M.J. 1974. "Pigs Are Our Hearts!: The Exchange Cycle among the Mae Enga of New Guinea." *Oceania* 44:165–203.

Radcliffe-Brown, A.R. 1952. *Structure and Function in Primitive Society*. London: Cohen & West.

Rappaport, Roy A. 1968. *Pigs Are the Ancestors: Ritual in the Ecology of a New Guinea People.* New Haven: Yale University Press.

Rubel, Paula G. and Abraham Rosman. 1978. *Your Own Pigs You May Not Eat: A Comparative Study of New Guinea Societies.* Chicago: The University of Chicago Press.

Strathern, Andrew. 1971a. "Wiru and Daribi Matrilateral Payments." *Journal of the Polynesian Society.* 80:449–62.

————. 1971b. *The Rope of Moka: Big-men and Ceremonial Exchange in Mount Hagen, New Guinea.* Cambridge: Cambridge University Press.

Turner, Victor. 1967. *The Forest of Symbols: Aspects of Mdembu Ritual.* Ithaca: Cornell University Press.

————. 1969. *The Ritual Process: Structure and Anti-structure.* Ithaca: Cornell University Press.

Watson, James B. 1977. "Pigs, Fodder, and the Jones Effect in Postipomoean New Guinea." *Ethnology.* 16:57–70.

Duke of York Shell Money:
A Mediator of Relationships

Dean and Dianne Moore

Introduction

Shell money is a traditional medium of exchange in the Duke of York/ Tolai areas.[1] It is used for buying garden produce, pigs, fish, or other commodities. Thus it is easy to assume that the Duke of York shell money is a currency like the other currencies of the world. But it is more than just a currency. This study suggests that shell money functions as a mediator of social relationships for the Duke of York people.

As a mediator stands between two people, so, by extension of meaning, it also stands between two things. Shell money in this sense can be said to stand between two people of the Tolai, encouraging effective relationships, or between the Tolai and their socioeconomic system. In either case shell money mediates the two aspects of Tolai life and in effect betters it for the sake of the members of the Tolai/Duke of York society.

Much has been written about the Duke of York and Tolai peoples. Brown (1910) was one of the first men to describe the shell money of New Britain. Salisbury (1970) focuses on the traditional use of shell money in relation to modern economic development in the area. He is also concerned with the relationship between shell money and politics. ToVaninara (1979) relates shell money to religious beliefs and practices. Many other scholars have contributed to the broad literature now available on the Tolai and their use of shell money.

---

1. The Duke of York people live on the Duke of York Islands group located between New Britain and New Ireland of the Bismarck archipelago in the St. George Channel. They are part of the East New Britain Province of Papua New Guinea. The Duke of York language is a member of the Southern Patpatar-Tolai language family. There are about ten thousand speakers of the language.

Shell Money Defined

Duke of York shell money is called *diwaara, tambu,* or *tabu.* In this paper the term *diwaara* will be used. *Diwaara* is a collection of the small *nassa immersa* shells. To make *diwaara* the Duke of York people begin by collecting these small shells, which are not found in their natural state on the Duke of York Islands, but are found principally on the north coast of New Britain near Nakanai. After they are collected or purchased, the shells are stored in bottles until they are processed. Sometimes they are bleached in the sun, giving them a whiteness and gloss that make them more valuable. Next they are strung onto shaven strips of cane. First the back or hump of the shell is pinched using a small pair of wire pliers. This forms a very small disk which is pushed onto the cane measuring one-quarter inch wide by one-eighth inch thick and about three feet long.

The cane strip may be split about one-eighth inch down from one end to allow the end of another strip of cane to be inserted onto it in an overlapping manner. In this way longer strands of *diwaara* can be made. These strands are measured in fathoms. One fathom is from one to one-and-a-half meters long. Five to ten fathoms are usually kept in loose coils for ease in handling and counting. Large rolls are sometimes made which hold between 300 and 500 fathoms.

Reason for exchange	Relationship involved	Amount of diwaara
Payment of fines	Individual-individual	Small (1/2-10 fathoms)
Bride price	Clan-clan	Large (250-300 fathoms)
Funeral feast	Living-deceased	Very large (up to 2000 fathoms)

Figure 1. *Diwaara* as mediator

Diwaara as Mediator

The basic role that *diwaara* fills in the Duke of York culture seems to be one of mediation: *diwaara* is used to establish new relationships and to maintain those already established. Its role is presented here in a hierarchy of relationships. Mediation occurs on three levels of the hierarchy, as shown on the chart in figure 1.

Diwaara exchanges are critical in relationships between individuals or groups of people. As the chart shows, the number of people involved increases as one moves to each successive level of the hierarchy. *Diwaara* acts as a mediator between two individuals on the lowest level of hierarchical interaction and between large groups on the highest level.

The amounts of *diwaara* exchanged in the mediation process is also associated hierarchically. When only two individuals are involved the amounts exchanged are small. These can range from very short sections of *diwaara* to ten fathoms in length. When two clans are involved the amount of *diwaara* exchanged is normally about 300 fathoms. The largest exchange involved is in the mediation between the living and the dead. Two thousand fathoms were exchanged at one funeral feast. It becomes evident that the more *diwaara* involved, the greater the importance of the mediation.

Individual Mediation

ToVaninara explicitly states the role of *diwaara* in individual mediation: in order to establish new relationships, reestablish older ones, or mend broken ones, shell money is the necessary and primary means. An offender who has committed adultery or theft, or caused severe conflicts, or participated in excessive argumentation, is required to compensate with shell money. In each of these cases, a peaceful relationship has been broken and has to be restored (1979:34). *Diwaara* is the mediator that enables such restoration of relationships to occur.

The first use of *diwaara* observed by the authors was in a village court case. A theft of coconuts had taken place and a village court was held to resolve the problem. Men and women were seated on opposite sides of the village area, and the village magistrate was seated on a mat under a large shade tree in the middle. A rather heated discussion ensued about the missing coconuts. Someone then presented five fathoms of *diwaara* to the magistrate. He in turn gave it to the victim of the theft. The issue was settled. The proper mediation had taken place, and the proper payment had been made and accepted.

Another type of fine in the Duke of York culture requiring *diwaara* payment involves in-law taboos. If a man passes too near to his mother-in-law or talks to her, he must give her a small amount of *diwaara*. This payment is a fine for not showing respect in avoiding her.

An illustration from Brown (1910) relates the big man's use of *diwaara* in mediation. Brown discusses the role of the big man historically and explains why only a wealthy man could fill the role as mediator since he owns the most shell money. In one case cited, Brown himself was owed several fathoms of *diwaara* by a big man. He went to see the debtor several times to collect it, but each time the man said he did not have it. Then Brown told the debtor not to trouble himself about it, but that he would take some *diwaara* to another big man of higher status. The debtor immediately said that he would be able to find enough *diwaara* to repay the debt. Had Brown given *diwaara* to the higher status man, it would have been ten percent of the amount which was owed to him. This big man would have then given Brown the repayment sought and later collected from the debtor the amount owed plus another ten per cent, netting twenty percent for his mediating efforts. To avoid paying this added ten percent, the debtor paid Brown immediately. Further investigation is still needed to determine whether this system is still in use today.

Clan-Level Mediation

Even as it is on the individual level, proper *diwaara* exchange is necessary to correctly establish and maintain clan-level relationships. Bride price exchange and the ceremony of "giving to the woman" illustrate this mediation.

The Duke of York people are clan exogamous. At a bride price exchange, the two clans involved have clear and distinct roles. The individuals in the bride's clan gather at or near the bride's home and wait for the groom's clan to arrive. The groom's clan gathers near the edge of the village or at some other central place nearby. When they assemble they collect the necessary *diwaara* from each clan member and place it in a decorated basket. Then they proceed amid shouts and conch shell fanfare to the place where the bride's clan has gathered. They are welcomed by the bride's clan with the usual gifts of betel nut. Each clan then sits as a group facing one another across a small open space. At this point there may be general speeches made by the leaders of each clan. The groom's clan then takes the collected *diwaara* out of the basket in ten-fathom coils and carries it across to the bride's family. They lay it on the ground in neat rows so that all can easily count the total amount being given. Three hundred fathoms is the average amount, but the authors have seen a case where the bride had been married before, and the price was only one hundred fifty fathoms. The bride's clan then collects the *diwaara* and returns it to the basket. More speeches follow to acknowledge that all is in order. After this the bride's clan gives final gifts of food and green bananas to the groom's clan. The groom's clan then departs, but the bride's clan remains to decide when to take the bride to her husband.

The custom of "giving to the woman" is another example of clan-level mediation involving *diwaara*. After a woman has been married and has her own family, her clan gives a celebration in her honor signifying that her household has been properly set up. The father of the woman organizes this exchange by sending *diwaara* to the woman's relatives and fellow clan members. They then accumulate various gift items to give to the woman that include a wide range of household goods, foods, and *diwaara*. Often these are purchased in bulk quantities. The authors have seen numerous rolls of cloth given in entire bolts for making dresses, curtains, or other items. The groom's clan also prepares gifts of food to give in return to the bride's clan. At the feast itself, there may be special dancing and singing which is also paid for in *diwaara* by the bride's clan. The clan leaders make speeches expressing the fulfillment of their obligations in the relationship.

The respect of the clan is important. The "giving to the woman" is a large display of clan wealth and by giving this feast the bride's clan gains much prestige and reinforces relationships with the groom's clan. Without this demonstration of prestige and respect the relationship between the two clans would be poor. Like a broken relationship between individuals, restoration would then be necessary between the two clans. The giving to the woman, then, assures proper relationships between the clans.

Living and Deceased Mediation

The relationship between the living and the deceased, or ancestral spirits, is the most important relationship in the Duke of York culture. Therefore, *diwaara* is more essential in the mediation of this relationship than in all other relationships, providing "a sure guarantee of proper relationships with the ancestral spirits" (ToVaninara 1979:37). The authors have been told that regardless of how much national currency or material property a Duke of York person has, that unless he has *diwaara* he is considered a poor man. The people desire large amounts of *diwaara* mainly for distribution at funeral feasts, or feasts held in honor of the ancestral spirits.

A funeral feast begins when young boys are sent to gather green coconuts to serve the visitors. The boys constantly chatter or whoop as they work. This is a signal to neighboring villages that a funeral feast is being prepared. The roasted pigs and other food are placed in a line near the house of the deceased. The visitors sit in a large square around the line of food. When the young boys enter the square behind a cover of dead coconut fronds, the host, usually some family member of the deceased, acknowledges their return with a short dance. The customary distribution of betel nut to all present is given as a welcoming gesture by the family of the deceased. This is followed by the first official part of the feast, the payment for the pigs. The host announces the price for each pig and the name of the owner. This amount of *diwaara* is then carried over to him in ten fathom units and laid at his feet. The average price per pig is about sixty fathoms, but one hundred fathoms is not rare.

The next item of business is to pay for any work done for the family of the deceased. At the time of death someone is appointed to keep a list of all work done and every worker who does it. The list is read at this time. All the persons named form a line to receive payment from the family members. If someone is absent or embarrassed a marker is placed in the line to signify his presence. Each family member then walks down the line breaking off short sections of *diwaara* and dropping them in front of the person or marker. The average length given is normally about six inches, but wealthy family members may give more.

Next, a general *diwaara* exchange takes place among the family members who have just paid the workers. The size of gifts at this point is between eighteen and twenty-four inches.

It is then time to carve the pigs. A list of the people selected to do this is called out. Since all the workers have already been paid, the appropriate amount of *diwaara* for this specific task is laid on each pig. The one who carves the pig will get this *diwaara*.

The feast ends with pigs being cut and distributed along with the coconuts and other food. There may be a short speech stating that all the wealth of the deceased has been properly distributed. The maternal nephew gets the largest share of the estate.

At the Duke of York funeral feast the mediation of relationships occurs between the worlds of the living and the dead. While there may or may not be overt interaction between them at the feast, the relationship between the living and the recent dead is now being established by the feast given in his honor. ToVaninara relates that contact with the ancestral spirits is made possible by means of *diwaara* (1979:35) and may be the most important mediation role assigned to it. The funeral feast provides a means to properly distribute the *diwaara* formerly owned by the deceased. It is now coming to the living by way of an ancestral spirit. Perhaps for this reason it is seen as sacred by the people.

Acquiring Shell Money

There is a close relationship between *diwaara*, mediation, and being a leader or big man in the Duke of York culture. The real leader is not necessarily the man appointed by the government but rather the man with the most *diwaara* (ToVaninara 1979:36). There are several ways that an aspiring leader can acquire large amounts of *diwaara*. They include selling produce in the market, rendering special services, becoming a trade or spiritual specialist, or owning a dance mask *(tuban)*.

Perhaps the least productive method of acquiring large amounts of shell money is to sell garden produce or fish. In the large vending market in Rabaul as well as in the smaller markets in the area, commodities ranging from betel nut and lime to piglets and chickens are sold, using both the national currency and *diwaara*. However, Salisbury (1966) points out that this is not a primary means of acquiring large amounts of *diwaara*.

Sometimes special services are rendered in order to acquire shell money, including such things as composing songs or dances which could be sold or performed for *diwaara*. If a big man is having a special party or feast, he may pay the composer for the privilege of performing the song or dance. The big man may himself learn the song or dance or he may simply pay the composer to perform the song or dance at the feast.

There is a highly developed system of trade specialists in the Duke of York society. There are skilled canoe builders, fish trap makers, carpenters, and so forth. As one learns a trade, *diwaara* is acquired through the sale of crafted items. There are also traditional spiritual specialists. Since *diwaara* is used as a means to contact the ancestral spirits, those men who have the required expertise would naturally acquire certain amounts of *diwaara* in their craft.

The most significant way to acquire wealth and its attendant power is to own or to raise one of the special dance masks *(tubuan),* of the men's secret society.[2] "Raising the mask" consists of preparing all the dance costumes involved in bringing it back to life and of hosting special dances or feasts related to the secret society. If the owner of the mask also wants to raise it, he alone pays for all the cost involved. This is done in *diwaara*. He can raise the mask for a period of a day or two weeks, depending on his own resources. If anyone wants to own a mask while it is alive, he must buy it from the one who raised it. The price for owning a mask ranges from one to three hundred fathoms, differing with the owners and special skills or powers of the mask. Thus, if ten men wanted to own a mask, the man who had raised it would be paid from one to three thousand fathoms.

The owner of the mask receives payment for all dances and other appearances or services rendered by the mask. If a nonmember of the society comes too near the mask or its sacred ground, a fine will be imposed and the mask will come to collect it from the person. Such visits are greatly feared by the people.

---

2. The Duke of York men's society is known as the Dukduk. For a fuller treatment of the society and its activities, see Brown (1910).

Conclusion

Diwaara, the traditional shell money of the Duke of York people, continues to thrive today, despite Papua New Guinea's strong national currency and some past area administrators who have attempted to discourage its use (Salisbury 1970:278). The use of *diwaara* in establishing new relationships and maintaining already established relationships shows its integral function in helping to fulfill interpersonal and intergroup obligations within the culture.

Diwaara is also used as payment in traditional methods of education, such as initiation ceremonies and learning skills from a specialist (ToVaninara 1979:41). One can therefore envision future possibilities of its use in other types of educational programs, both national and local.

References

Brown, George. 1910. *Melanesians and Polynesians.* London: Macmillan.

Salisbury, Richard. 1970. *Vunamami.* Melbourne: University Press.

ToVaninara, Caspar G., MSC. 1979. "Tambu: Traditional Sacred Wealth." In *Powers, Plumes, and Piglets,* ed. by Norman C. Habel. Australian Association for the Study of Religions, pp. 33–44.

Mami Reveals Dynamic Kwanga Social Structure

Takashi Manabe

Introduction

According to French and Bridle (1978), among the six varieties of yams found in Papua New Guinea, only two are important as the staple food of New Guineans. They are the greater yam, *yam-tru* (Tok Pisin), and the lesser yam *mami*. In Kwanga[1] society the lesser yam is the more important. It has importance for the villagers, not so much for its food value, but rather for its ceremonial value in food exchange in Tambaran cult activities.

Linda Polley (1980) reports that the study of the chicken among the Mundu people of Sudan, Africa, gave helpful insights into understanding Mundu society. Chicken is used not only as a food and an element in economic exchange but it also plays a part in social relationships such as friendship as well as in spiritual aspects of the Mundu such as the appeasement of spirits and magic. *Mami* functions similarly in Kwanga society. By tracing the flow of *mami* from one location to another and considering its function in each aspect of Kwanga society in terms of who is involved and for what purpose related activities are performed, one develops a dynamic social map of the society.

---

1. Mr. and Mrs. Manabe started a vernacular language project in August 1978 under the auspices of the Summer Institute of Linguistics (SIL) in the village of Yupanakor, located to the southwest of Maprik in the Maprik subdistrict of the East Sepik Province. A dialect of the Kwanga language is spoken in Yupanakor and its seven surrounding villages.

The data used in this paper were collected during their residence in Yupanakor village from August 1978 through May 1981. Language assistants and other villagers contributed to the collection of data and provided a check on their accuracy.

Tuzin (1972) presents a thesis that yam = body, yam = penis, and yam = pride. These three levels of symbolism involving the yam in Ilahita Arapesh, a neighboring group to the Kwanga, may be present in any given expression of yam-oriented belief or behavior. In Kwanga society, however, *mami* = female body.

Ceremonial man is conceptualized by the Kwanga as male. *Mami* is conceptualized as female. This effectively excludes woman from ceremonial participation since the male-female pairing is complete without her. She is therefore declared ceremonially unclean since any involvement with her would signify a kind of ceremonial fornication. At the height of the ceremonial activities, the most important fertility ceremony is performed between the man and the *mami*. Thus the *mami* is impregnated and, when fed to women and pigs, assures fertility much as artificial insemination does to animals in Western societies.

In this paper the *mami* is traced from its mythological origins through the social system and village activities including gardening, the exchange system, and into a summary of the system of Kwanga basic values.

Mythological Origin

Ancestral stories, i.e., legends and myths which have been transmitted orally for generations, are especially valuable for the understanding of a society where people still seriously retain their traditional values. The Kwanga is one such society. Following is an abridged Tambaran[2] story told by a middle-aged man who has gone through one stage of initiation.

1. Long ago there was a girl and her grandparent in the village. 2. The girl climbed a tulip tree and went up and up nearer to the sky and said, "Grandparent, I will try to point to the sky with a twig." 3. The grandparent said, "No, you cannot do it, lest the sky hold you." 4. But the girl did not listen to the grandparent and she tried to point to the sky with the twig, but all of a sudden she was held fast by the sky and the twig dropped down to the ground. 5. She was swaying from side to side, while her legs were held by the sky. 6. A little later, when her parents came, her grandparent told them to make a fence around the tulip tree. 7. So, the father cut *pitpit* and built a fence around the tree. 8. Eventually the body of the girl rotted and fell to the ground. 9. After awhile, a sprout came out of it and it grew like

---

2. According to Mead (1973), *Tambaran* is: cult objects and supernaturals associated with the division between adult males and females and children, which stresses the hypothesized procreative (or parental) role of the males versus the females. The word may apply to a house in which objects forbidden to woman are kept (either individually, clan, moiety, or village owned); noise makers and musical instruments; beings to whose reality the sounds attest for the benefit of the uninitiated; as well as to other objects used in the theatrical presentations of the cult.

a *mami*. 10. It grew bigger and bigger and its leaves became dry, ready for harvest. 11. The father then went to the bush to hunt, and then to the river to get water. 12. After this, he dug the *mami* and brought it back and told his wife to cook it with the meat and the water. 13. After she cooked, he ate it and slept. 14. While he was sleeping, his testicles became big. 15. In this way the girl went into the testicles. 16. He went to and fro in this way for awhile. 17. One day he decided to go to the garden to plant *mami*. 18. Carrying *mami* in a string bag hung on his shoulder, he came to the edge of the village and the girl came down out of him. 19. Then she carried the *mami* in the string bag hung on her head. 20. In the garden he planted *mami* while the girl was clearing away brush. 21. After planting the *mami*, the two came back to the village. The girl had collected firewood and was carrying it in the string bag hung on her head. 22. When they came to the edge of the village, the girl went up into his testicles again, and he carried the firewood in the string bag hung on his shoulder back to the village. 23. They went on doing this day after day. 24. One day he went to pick up breadfruit. 25. He climbed the tree and he plucked a fruit and threw it a long way in one direction, and then another a long way in another direction, and another in another direction, and said to the girl "Go and get them." 26. While she was going to get the fruit a long distance away, he said some words to the stick and hung it on the tree and left the place. 27. She came back and called him, and the stick responded, "Here I am." 28. It went on like that for awhile, but she began to wonder whether he really was up there. 29. So she climbed the tree and called him, and the stick responded. 30. Very disappointed, she broke the stick into pieces and threw them away and came down from the tree and went to an area of *bochika* grass and sat crying. 31. While she was crying, men who were involved in the third stage of initiation (*ambwa*) came and saw her and took her secretly to the Tambaran house (men's cult house). 32. Then they built a small room for her to stay. 33. And every man brought a cup of soup which his wife cooked and gave it to her. 34. Then they went out again and brought in necklaces and pendants and decorated her. 35. And so she stayed in the Tambaran house. 36. One day, two women came and climbed a coconut tree which was beside the Tambaran house. 37. They plucked a coconut and said, "Why have they been bringing in soup with cups? What happened to those necklaces and pendants? They must have hidden a woman in that house." 38. The old man who was watching over the house while the men went into the bush for the *ambwa* initiation ritual tried to stop the women from throwing the coconut by exposing his penis and putting ash on it. 39. But it was no use, the women threw the coconut down onto the house, and the coconut went through the roof and hit the woman and killed her. 40. Then the old man wept. 41. When the men came back from the bush, he said to them, "Your women are bad. A little while ago, they came and plucked a coconut and killed your woman with it. I exposed my penis and I put ash on it, but it was no use." 42. So they secretly took the body of the woman and dug a hole and buried her. 43. Then they made charcoal out of a *mambilong* tree, and brought their sons in to the Tambaran house, leaving their daughters with their wives. 44. Next they rubbed the bodies of their sons with the charcoal so that their skin became deep black. 45. Then they said to their wives, "You come and look at us! You are good wives and we are good husbands. You are with our daughters and we are with our sons." 46. After that the men continued to stay in the Tambaran house for some time. 47. Then they came out and said to their wives, "You look at us! You are good wives and we are good husbands. We will change into flying foxes." 48. After they changed into flying foxes they said to their wives, "Look at us." 49. Then they sang this song. (The story teller demonstrates by singing them the song.) 50. That is the end of my story.

This story of the old men of the Kwanga suggests that bush spirits (*masalai*) representing the sky provide the ultimate backdrop for the interaction of male and female. At first the girl becomes *mami* and then *mami* becomes symbolically female. Then the man becomes ceremonial man and thus symbolically male. The interaction of the male penis and the female as *mami* provide the foundation for fertility among the Kwanga. Figure 1 summarizes the primary interactions of the story.

The story teller focuses on the basic opposition between the two main participants in confrontation, i.e., the man and the girl. In order to produce the high drama and significance of the tale, the story teller skillfully employs a technique of off-staging a main participant in various places in the story as, for example, in line 6, the grandparent, in lines 24–30, the man, and in lines 36–39, the girl (see fig. 1). What is more revealing is the fact that all the confrontations except for three cases (4–5, 6, and 40–42) are the confrontation between male and female from the male point of view which reflects well the male-dominant Kwanga society. The two confrontations in 6 and 40–42 are not in the thematic flow of the story, because they are used merely as connecting what precedes to what follows. The confrontation between sky and girl (4–5) can be understood as male-female confrontation, sky representing the male. But this confrontation can be further understood as providing the power source for men for the fulfillment of male ego. Therefore, sky can be interpreted as *masalai* 'bush spirit'. And *masalai* here functions as the originator of making women subservient in the society and the provider of power to men. This power is transmitted from girl to *mami* (9–13), to man (14–16), and to Tambaran men (31–35). It is made available only through men planting *mami* (24–30), in incantation (24–30), and in sorcery (43–49), men changing into flying foxes.

Sentences	Confrontation	Notes
1–3	grandparent—girl	
4–5	sky—girl	the sky: the power of *masalai*
6	grandparent—father	grandparent off-stage
7–8	father—girl	
9–13	father—*mami*	girl changes into *mami*
14–16	man—girl	focus change from father to man
17–23	man—girl	man and girl in harmonious *mami* gardening
24–30	man—girl	man off-stage (man performs incantation)
31–35	Tambaran men—girl	Tambaran men and girl in harmonious living
36–39	old man—two women	girl off-stage
40–42	old man—Tambaran men	
43–49	Tambaran—women men	Tambaran men and women, harmonious living exhorted. Tambaran men changes into flying foxes.
50	End	

Figure 1. Summary of confrontations in story

A second story links natural woman, i.e., not "female," with the pig. In the "Pig Story," the Kwanga explain that pigs came into being a long time ago when a woman who was the first wife of a certain man, bore piglets and she herself became a mother pig. The story validates the present reality in Kwanga society in which women take care of pigs. At the same time, the male point of view, that of considering women as the same rank as pigs, is reflected in the story. In the first story, woman is symbolized as *mami*, and in the second as pig.

Social System

Kwanga society is seen as a dynamic, living whole in which members of the society relate to one other in unique ways, not only to fulfill their basic needs such as metabolism, reproduction, protection, and the maintenance of the society in equilibrium, but also to produce the highest

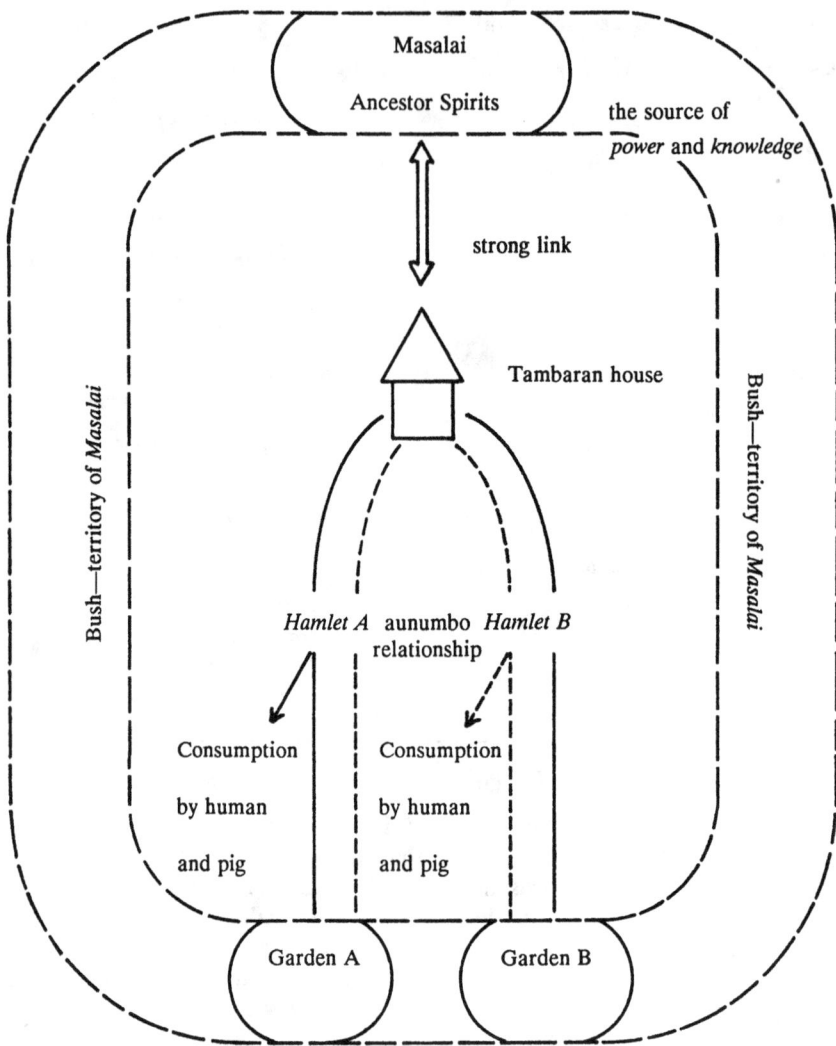

Figure 2. *Mami* flow diagram between two exchange hamlets

fulfillment in creative expression which reflects their ideologies and value system. *Mami* is the single most important staple in the Kwanga society and can be observed throughout the culture to reflect its internal dynamic. The *mami* flow diagram reveals the core structure of the society (fig. 2).

According to this diagram, the Kwanga society is described as one where the central social relationship which constitutes an exchange system is between two hamlets. *Mami* is the vital object which is exchanged between the two hamlets in an endless cycle through the two main ceremonial locations, the Tambaran house and the garden where *mami* is grown. Tambaran house is a place in which *mami* are empowered and men receive special power and knowledge from *masalai* 'bush spirits' and ancestral spirits. Garden is a place where empowered *mami* are planted by men who have received secret knowledge to produce symbolic fertility and the increase of their wealth.

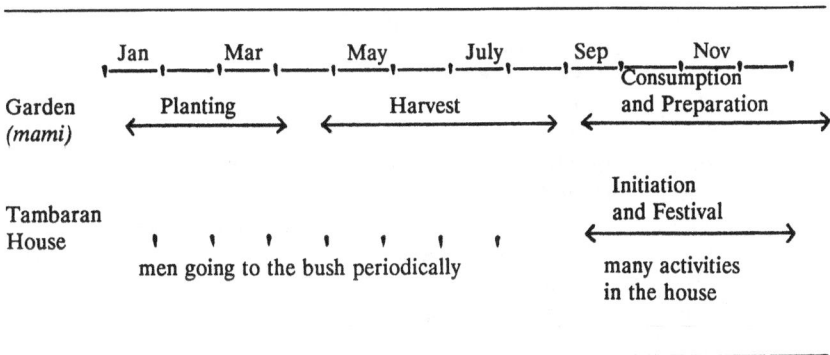

Figure 3. *Mami*-related activities in a year

Village Activities

Figure 3 demonstrates that the Kwanga society is concerned with *mami*-related activities throughout the year. Men, women, and children are busy planting, tending, and harvesting *mami* most of the year. They are busy the rest of the time with the preparation for planting *mami* in the succeeding year and with activities involving initiation and celebration. Adult men, i.e., those who have been initiated, need to go into the bush periodically as a group to ensure the good growth of *mami*. During the festival season they are especially busy doing this.

Gardening and the Family

The nuclear family consists of a man, his wives, and their immediate offspring. The hamlet is a small group of people who occupy a specified area of land holdings. Often they are closely related and form an extended family composed of a family head, married sons, and their spouses and children (Loving 1977).

Of all the crops raised by the Kwanga, such as *mami*, yam, banana, taro, sugar cane, bean, corn, and various edible greens, the most important is *mami*. All the other crops are secondary in importance.

The sharp division of labor between men, women and children, and between the initiated and the uninitiated, is observed in the garden-related tasks. Men are responsible for cutting down the trees of a newly chosen spot in the bush for a garden, while women and children are responsible for cutting the small branches off the trees. When the cut trees dry, they are burned and the spot is cleared to make the garden. The men build a fence around the garden. All the crops and vegetables are then planted by men and women together, except *mami* and yam (hereafter the word *mami* includes yam, since in the mind of the people yam is considered in the same class as *mami*). *Mami* is planted only by the men who have secret knowledge of planting it. They have to obey strictly some taboos during the period when they are planting *mami*. They believe that the good production of *mami* is directly related to fertility in their offspring and in pigs, which are the vital means to achieve prestige in the society. They pray to *masalai* and ancestral spirits whose power is believed to be essential for good production, and then they plant *mami* (see fig. 2).

Tending the garden is primarily the work of women, although men and children help in various stages of the work. However, only the men hang the vines of *mami* on their supporting poles or sticks. When there is not enough rain, it is the men's responsibility to perform a rain dance ceremony. Only the men who have the secret knowledge of this ceremony can pray to *masalai* for rain.

All the members of a nuclear family can join in the time of rejoicing at harvest. Only adult men who are qualified to perform the "digging *mami*" ceremonies are allowed to dig *mami*.

It is clear from the above discussion that men in association with *masalai* and ancestral spirits are in the position of having control of the total process of *mami*-related gardening. This reflects the importance of *mami* in Kwanga society. The Trend Dichotomy and Trend Prestige Achieved orientation of the society (see p. 56) is manifested through men's monopolized right to perform *mami*-related ceremonies to get power from *masalai* and ancestral spirits.

Exchange System

The Kwanga society has produced an exchange system, *aunumbo,* which is designed to last forever. The core of the system is the pairing together of hamlets as exchange partners. The whole village is paired in this way with no one excluded. *Aunumbo* is a pervasive system which functions like the engine of a car. Individual activities in a nuclear family, as well as whole village activities (such as Tambaran cult activities) and festivals, are motivated by this vital social interrelationship system of the society.

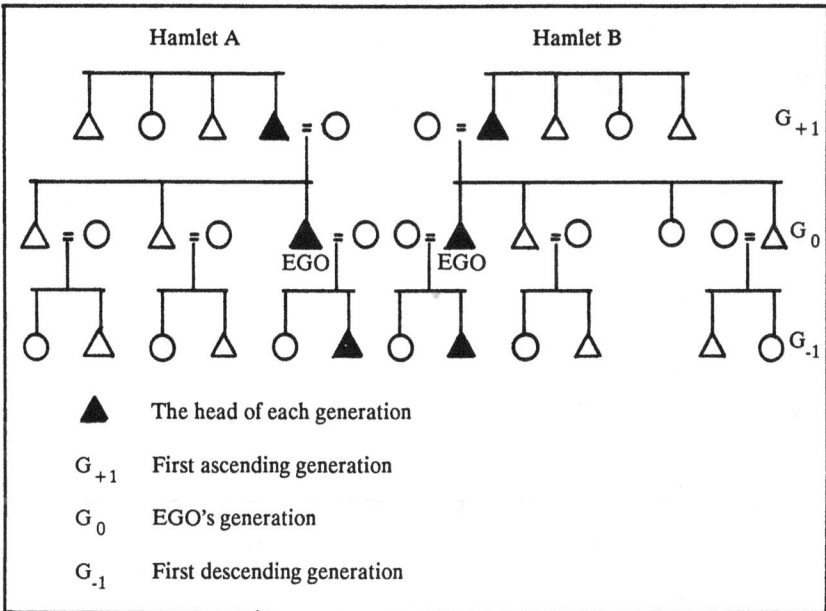

Figure 4. *Aunumbo* relationship

Aunumbo requires two groups, hamlet A and hamlet B (see figs. 2 and 4). Each hamlet usually consists of three generations. Same-generation brother-brother relationship is primary, and the father-son relationship is secondary in this patrilineal society. The residents of the married male EGO's hamlet include his parents, his wife and children, the families of his father's brothers (whom he also calls "father"), his brothers' families, and his unmarried sisters. In this society where life expectancy is rather short, EGO's second ascending and descending generations are not considered (see fig. 4).

The two hamlets in *aunumbo* relationship have obligations to fulfill for each other. They constantly exchange food (cooked pig, *mami,* etc.) and labor for mutual benefit, which contribute to strengthening or deepening their relationship. Two very important activities are performed by the two hamlets in *aunumbo* relationship, the fertility rite and the transmission of secret knowledge. Both of these activities are the core of the Tambaran cult.

Names of initiation ceremonies	Praying to masalai or ancestral spirits	Naming of initiates
1. *naku*	X (?)	X (?)
2. *ambwa ke*	X (?)	0
3. *ambwa*	0	0
4. *kwari*	0	0
5. *minja*	0	0
6. *nakuhopo minja*	0	0

Figure 5. Names of kinds of initiation ceremonies

The fertility rite is the essential activity which is denoted in figure 2. For Kwanga men, *mami* is more than just food. It is the vital medium through which supernatural power is transfused into human beings and pigs for their fertile production. In this male-dominant society, a man can achieve his prestige only by getting more wives, offspring, and pigs, thus producing more *mami* which is the symbol of fertility. Hamlets A and B in *aunumbo* relationship help each other in the fertility rite. When a man in hamlet A is going through an initiation, the members of hamlet B are responsible to provide enough *mami* for hamlet A. These *mami* are carried into the Tambaran house by the members of hamlet B for the fertility rite and then carried out by the members of hamlet A for their use, i.e., consumption and planting. It is believed that these *mami*, empowered through *masalai* and ancestral spirits, are essential for the fertile production of food (*mami* being central), offspring, and pigs. hamlet A, which received *mami* this time, needs to reciprocate by giving *mami* to the members of hamlet B, when another stage of initiation will be held the next time. Thus hamlet A and hamlet B in *aunumbo* relationship are providing mutual help by exchanging *mami*, the symbol of fertility.

Transmission of secret knowledge is another core activity performed by the two hamlets in *aunumbo* relationship. The Kwanga society has produced a complicated system of initiation ceremonies. Through them a massive amount of secret knowledge is transmitted from the older generation to the younger. Secret knowledge ranges from techniques of making baskets, spears, carvings, or musical instruments, to that of performing ceremonies or sorcery. There are six kinds, or stages, of initiation ceremony which occur in the Tambaran house. Figure 5 lists them in terms of name, whether a specific praying session to *masalai* is offered, and whether naming of initiates is performed.

Through the initiation ceremonies in the Tambaran house, not only vast amounts of secret knowledge are passed down from older to younger generations, but also certain fertility rites are performed in each session of initiation.

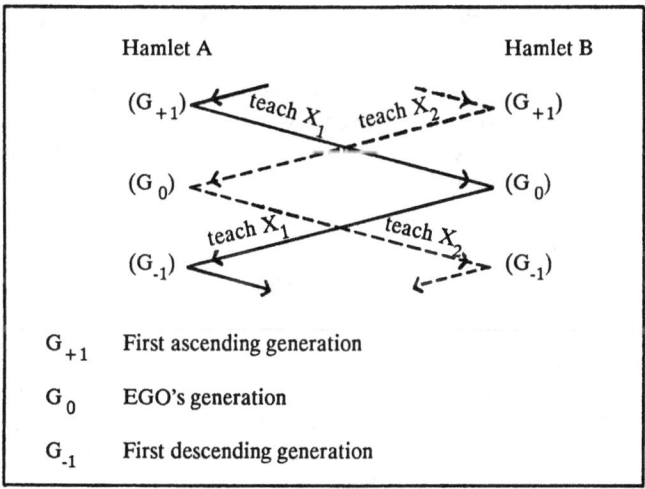

Figure 6. Transmission of secret knowledge

Aunumbo social relationship plays a vital role in this area, too. Because as figure 6 indicates, two hamlets in *aunumbo* relationship form the basic social unit in the whole village event of Tambaran initiations and festivals.

Figure 6 deals with an example of two of the six kinds of initiation listed in figure 5, here named X_1 and X_2. Concerning X_1, G_{+1} of hamlet A teaches what they were taught by G_{+2} of hamlet B to G_0 of hamlet B. However, some years later G_0 of hamlet B needs to repay G_{-1} of hamlet A by teaching what they received from G_{+1} of hamlet A. X_2 is also handed down in the same manner, from G_{+1} of hamlet B to G_0 of hamlet A, and then some years later from G_0 of hamlet A to G_{-1} of hamlet B. In this way all of the six kinds of initiation secrets are handed down from the older generation to the younger through the mutual education system of the two hamlets in the *aunumbo* relationship. Chronological sequence of the reciprocal handing down of initiation secrets is indicated by circled numbers in the diagram.

Another important activity occurring in each stage of initiation is that of naming. A set of names is attached to each initiation and they are handed down from generation to generation. As the older generation teaches the younger, so the names previously given to the older are handed down to the younger following each initiation. And at the same time the ones who give names also change their names, choosing their new names from among those of their ancestors. Thus, logically considered, a man after learning and teaching all the six kinds of initiation needs to change his own name twelve times! It is understood that his twelfth name will remain his name for the rest of his life, since he has reached the highest stage or rank which his society can offer. He is the *mekupu naha* 'the truly old man'.[3]

This naming system, as well as the system of handing down secret knowledge, both support the proposed Kwanga society cognitive style (see next section), i.e., the male dominant society where every man is required to achieve his prestige by going through each stage of initiation.

Kwanga Basic Values

The corporate cognitive style or pattern of the Kwanga society as a whole can be described in terms of its basic values. This is suggested by the cognitive styles model called Basic Values developed by Marvin K. Mayers (1978). This hypothesized deep-structure cognitive style of the Kwanga society is seen as a powerful tool to explain the verbal and non-verbal behavior of the society, especially as it relates to mami.

The hierarchy of cognitive style[4] presented in figure 7 is proposed as representative of Kwanga society.

---

3. There are two other kinds of names in the Kwanga society. One is the village name. Everyone is given a name when he or she is born. If a baby is female, the name given to her will be her name for the rest of her life. But if a baby is male, he will reach a certain stage of his life when his name will be changed into a name of initiation. The third naming system, the Christian, was introduced by the mission working in the area.

4. The terms used in this section are defined in Mayers 1978.

Figure 7 presents three cognitive style doublets. These show the Kwanga society to be male dominated, with a sharp distinction between men and women within a context of the highest perceived value of this society, that of men achieving prestige. A series of basic oppositions revealing Trend Dichotomy pervades the Kwanga culture: (1) male vs. female; (2) man vs. women-plus-pig; (3) spirit world vs. man's world; (4) Tambaran house vs. garden; (5) hamlet A vs. hamlet B; and (6) men's work vs. women's work.

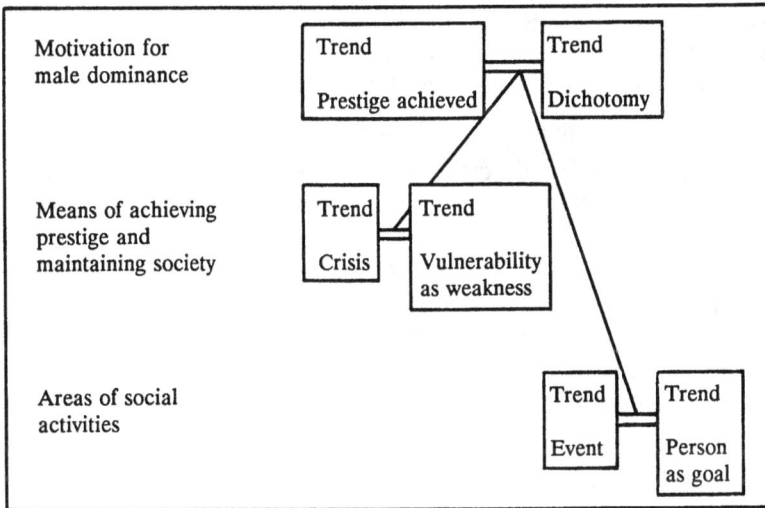

Figure 7. Cognitive style of Kwanga society

In order to achieve the highest prestige, men strive for power and authority (crisis) from supernatural beings and ancestral spirits. The society utilizes covert social sanctions, e.g., sorcery (vulnerability seen as weakness), against those who violate the rules of proper behavior and attempt to achieve prestige in socially unacceptable ways. In the "Wasi Story," it is told that the awful *wasi* sorcery was originated by one of the ancestral women who ate the flesh of her grandchildren. However, in the present day Kwanga society, it is men who eat dead human flesh and practice *wasi* sorcery. The seeming contradiction is resolved by realizing that the male dominant society needs a hidden means of killing one's enemies or competitors so that only limited numbers of men will be qualified to achieve the highest prestige. But the men cannot admit the disadvantageous fact that this awful sorcery is learned by men in their Tambaran house from which they exercise legitimate authority over the village people.

The virtues of generosity (event) and mutual aid (person as goal) are important to the Kwanga, but in relation to the other values, these are the lowest in the hierarchy.

Conclusion

Mami 'lesser yam' is the most important item in Kwanga society. By tracing the flow of *mami* from one location to another in the Kwanga society and considering its function within each aspect of the society in terms of who is involved and for what purpose related activities are performed, one develops a dynamic social map of the society.

The importance of *mami* can be seen in four ways:

(1) It distinguishes female from male and becomes sacred object-as-female in the Tambaran house. This excludes the woman and in essence declares her unclean.

(2) It is the central symbol of fertility. When the specific fertility ceremony is performed on the *mami*, it becomes impregnated. Woman and pig thereby become artificially inseminated when they eat the *mami* used in the ceremony.

(3) It is the primary object of exchange for two hamlets in the *aunumbo* relationship.

(4) It is the dominant object for family garden involvement. It is vital for men in the ceremonial garden, and for women in the family village garden.

Kwanga society thus revolves around basic oppositions (dichotomy). The focus of authority is in the male (prestige achieved). Witchcraft, or sorcery, is used to reduce the number of big men as leaders (crisis), yet there is no desire on the men's part to reveal their involvement in sorcery since they are also the legitimate leaders (vulnerability as weakness). The society as event and person as goal makes an informal and spontaneous setting for village life to be carried out as it revolves around *mami*.

References

French, Bruce and Celia Bridle. 1978. *Food Crops of Papua New Guinea*. Vudal College of Agriculture with the assistance of funds provided by New Zealand Aid Programme.

Loving, Richard, ed. 1977. *Technical Studies Handbook—Anthropology Section.* SIL: Ukarumpa, Papua New Guinea.

Mayers, Marvin K. 1978. "The Basic Values: An Introductory Manual." Preliminary edition not for publication.

————. 1981. "Sociolinguistics Course Class Materials and Notes." SIL–University of Texas at Arlington graduate course, held at Ukarumpa, Papua New Guinea.

Mead, Margaret. 1973. "An Examination of Major Themes of the Sepik District, Papua New Guinea." *Ninth International Congress of Anthropological and Ethnological Sciences.*

Olson, Michael L. 1974. "The Semantics of Barai Kinship and Social Organization." *Kinship studies in Papua New Guinea,* ed. by R. Daniel Shaw, p.53–68. SIL.

Pence, Alan R. 1974. "The Nature of Kunimaipa Kinship Terms." *Kinship Studies in Papua New Guinea,* ed. by R. Daniel Shaw, p.69–77. SIL.

Polley, Linda. 1980. "Fowl Play: Notes on the Value and Use of Chicken in the Mundu Society." Unpublished manuscript.

Tuzin, Donald F. 1972. "Yam Symbolism in the Sepik: An Interpretative Account." *Southwestern Journal of Anthropology,* 28:230–54.

Whiting, John W. M. 1951. *Becoming a Kwoma: Teaching and Learning in a New Guinea Tribe.* New Haven: Yale University.

The Interrelationship of Taboo and Kinship as the Cohesive Agent of Saniyo-Hiyowe Society

Ronald K. Lewis

Introduction

Saniyo-Hiyowe[1] social structure seems loose and somewhat haphazard. Its behavioral profile could be drawn as trend-event, trend-holistic, and trend-noncrisis (Mayers 1978:22–25). Yet solidarity and cohesion are manifested in the society. What makes the Saniyo-Hiyowe people function as a society? What is the cohesive agent which gives the society its solidarity?

I propose that kinship is the cohesive agent which ties the Saniyo-Hiyowe society together, and that the taboo system which operates within the

---

1. The Saniyo-Hiyowe are a small group of semi-nomadic people, inhabiting the swamplands of the upper reaches of the Wogamous, April, and Leonard Schultz Rivers in a latitudinal plain. Linguistically, Saniyo-Hiyowe is the most western member of the Sepik Hills language family. The society takes its subsistence from sago, supplementing it with a primitive horticulture of bananas, pineapple, papaya, taro, squash, and cucumbers. Gathering edible foodstuffs from the rain forest contributes to the diet of the people. Hunting and fishing provide protein in their diet.

The elevation of the area is from 300–400 feet above sea level. Until recently most of the hamlets were built on knolls or hills interspersed throughout the swamps. (The word for mountain and for village or hamlet are the same.) The average yearly rainfall is nearly 200 inches. The drainage basin for the Wogamous River is small, resulting in a rapid rise and fall of the river level.

The population of the two major dialects is approximately 600. The group is strategically located in that the surrounding languages have populations of from 40 to 150. Out of necessity and survival these other language groups have learned Saniyo-Hiyowe and are utilizing it as their trade language. There is a large percentage of intermarriage among these groups.

61

kinship system gives the society its solidarity. The two systems, or networks, work together to control the behavior of individuals within the society.

There are four types of relationships in which the Saniyo-Hiyowe interact: (1) consanguineal, (2) affinal, (3) friendship, and (4) spirit-world. Kinship is established and extended beyond the consanguineal relationship and becomes the element of solidarity within the society.

The taboo system operates within each type of kinship relationship and is the phenomenon that unifies the society. By taboo, I am referring to that which is forbidden, but the term may be applied to any sort of prohibition (Radcliffe-Brown 1952:133). For the Saniyo-Hiyowe taboos are an integral part of life. Their function is, in effect, to control the society. Taboos cover three major areas of life: food, personal relationships, and the spirit world.

Following is a description of the major types of relationship and a development of the taboo system as it occurs within each relationship of the society.

Consanguineal Relationships

The vertical limit of consanguineal relationships is five generations. Anyone before the limit of memory is considered an ancestor. The Saniyo-Hiyowe are patrilineal in descent and patrilocal in residence. The terms for parallel cousins and siblings are merged. Cross cousins of the same sex are merged bilaterally. Cross cousins of the opposite sex, however, display characteristics similar to those of the Omaha system. A male, for example, calls his mother's brother's daughter "mother," and she in turn, refers to him as "son." Father's sister's daughter and EGO's sister's daughter are merged by the same term. The terms for EGO's brother's children and EGO's children are merged into terms for sons and daughters (Townsend 1969:148–50).

Although the society is patrilineal and patrilocal, one must not discount the influence women have in the society. If a wife has a strong personality or comes from a powerful lineage, the couple may decide to live in the vicinity of her family. The greatest factor in determining one's residence, however, is whatever lineage connection offers the most advantages. If an individual can discover a kin relationship in a hamlet in which he wishes to live, he will use that relationship to establish his residence. Since the lines of inheritance pass through the male line, an individual can claim access to goods, services, and lands owned by any of the men he calls father.

Food is by far the most prevalent entity in the taboo system and is called into play primarily in regard to consanguineal relationships. There are food taboos relating to pregnancy, the postpartum period, sexual relations, and death. In pregnancy, for example, the expectant mother is forbidden to eat pork, certain birds, marsupials, and sago until several months following the birth of her baby. When a close relative dies, certain foods such as pork, sago, and squash are forbidden until the first of three memorial feasts occur. Men are restricted from eating certain species of rats, snakes, lizards, bats, turtles, and the crown pigeon. When a hunter shoots or captures one of these animals which is taboo to him, he will bring it to his wife or another person within his hamlet who is allowed to eat it. Women are restricted from eating certain species of birds and marsupials. Children below puberty are restricted from eating the hornbill, cockatoo, bats, and snakes.

Nearly every variety of food is taboo to some person or category of people. Two groups of people seem to be relatively free from the taboo system—those who are too old to produce their own food, and those who are too young. Since they do not produce food, they tend to eat whatever they can secure.

Food taboos function as a control of the population in relation to available food resources. Although it deprives an individual of a particular food, it controls the population in terms of how many people the land will support. Due in part to the additional burden of food taboos, infants and those already weakened by illness have a higher death rate in times of food shortage than in times of plenty.

Food taboos also provide a mechanism for sharing food outside the nuclear family. The meat of pigs, cassowaries, and large marsupials is distributed not only within the hunter's family, but also among members of the community, crossing family boundaries. If a family should include a good hunter, the meat he secures goes to families who may not have successful hunters. Food taboos also strengthen the bonds between people of the same age and sex. When an age mate is restricted by some taboo, others of the set will rally around him and provide him with food he is able to eat.

The functions of consanguineal kin relationships include the acquisition of land, the training of children, the passing of ritual knowledge, and the primary source for bride wealth.

Acquisition of Land

Each lineage controls certain areas of land, divided among its living members. Any lineage member may utilize sago palms or build a garden located within his lineage territory. Within the boundaries of the area controlled by the lineage, an individual may plant or mark certain sago palms for himself or his family. This territory is also the private hunting ground for the members of his particular lineage. For example, if a pig has been killed by someone from a distant lineage, it is brought into the hamlet and shared among the members of the lineage who control the land. Although the hunter may take some of the meat with him to his own hamlet,[2] most of the meat will stay in the local hamlet. If someone were to remove an animal without the knowledge of the lineage heads, serious consequences would occur.

Training of Children

The training of children is an integral part of Saniyo-Hiyowe life style and is the responsibility of close consanguineal kin. Beginning with the nuclear family, fathers train their sons in various skills needed for providing shelter, goods, and protection. At approximately two or three years of age, boys are allowed to play with bush knives and axes. They are continually swinging them, cutting and slashing until they are able to handle them with ease. In addition, they are instructed in the preparation and use of fire. They learn to wrap certain foods in leaves and cook them in the open fire. While the boys still quite young, their fathers give them small bows with a few straw arrows. Becoming proficient with the bows requires a number of years of shooting grasshoppers, fruit from the trees, bobbing fruit in a stream, or anything else they deem shootable. Young boys often go with their fathers into the jungle to acquire knowledge of jungle lore: what is edible, how to traverse swamps and track animals, and which trees are good for house building or canoes. They also learn how to build temporary shelters and dugout canoes and become proficient in handling canoes.

Girls remain with their mothers, helping them and learning the role of women in the society. Since sago is the chief staple, preparation of sago starch is by far the most important task for girls to learn. Every stage of preparation must be learned, from the felling of the palm to the making of sago pudding. Girls are taught to be good wives and mothers as well as what is expected of them in their kinship roles. The mother/daughter relationship is like that of master to apprentice—a daughter sitting at her mother's feet and assimilating knowledge of the roles she will be expected to play. Girls learn that since menstrual blood is a dangerous substance, sexual intercourse is taboo during menstruation (cf. Meigs). They also learn that during pregnancy taboos restrict them in terms of what they

---

2. The young hunter himself may be forbidden to eat the animal which he has killed. The food taboos within the society dictate his actions and thus promote the sharing of food equally throughout the community (Townsend 1969:122–25).

can eat and do. Both sago and pork will be removed from their diet, leaving them with a limited supply of protein. They will be also forbidden to prepare sago because of the possibility of contaminating it for men. Sexual intercourse will be taboo for the same reason. Should a woman have intercourse after she becomes pregnant, the result will be twins, one of which must be killed before she leaves the birth hut.

Passing of Ritual Knowledge

In addition to training children in the ways of life, specialized training is imparted to certain children by their parents or specialists. Ritual magic for hunting, dispersing rain, curing illness, communicating with the spirits, and exorcism is passed down to selected individuals. These training sessions are done in the secrecy of the men's house. In addition to their training, young men who are passing into manhood are placed under certain taboos for the duration of their initiation rites. They are completely secluded from the women. For about two weeks all pork and sago are restricted. The older men secure food, cook it, and give it to the young initiates. All the evil influence of women is totally removed from the young men, as women are supposed to drain the strength and virility from men.

Primary Source of Bride Wealth

Consanguineal relationships are a primary source of bride wealth. The underlying concept of bride wealth is the binding together of two kin groups through marriage. A young man intending to marry must go to his consanguineal kin and secure wealth to present to his fiancée's family. This causes the young man to depend on his family, building a chain of obligation which ideally should eventually be paid back and which ties the young man to those who provide the bride wealth for a long time. Bride wealth also provides security for the contributors when they become too old to work sago. As a man grows older, younger men borrow bride wealth from him and he accrues a reserve of prestige based on outstanding obligations.

Affinal Relationships

A second network of relationships is established by marriage. These relationships are generally between communities or at least between lineages. While marriages within a lineage do occasionally occur, the ideal marriage is with a person outside of one's lineage. It is generally considered foolish to marry a kinsman because if you had not, you might have been able to receive bride wealth by arranging her marriage to someone else. There is also a fear that the children of such a marriage will die.

As affinal relationships are extended to other lineages and communities, a man builds banks of obligation with his in-laws, again tying into the security system for his old age when he may cash in when in need. Affinal relationships also extend lines of alliance. Although the need for alliances has somewhat diminished as a result of government control, the people are hesitant to disregard the alliance system. Fear of raids and attacks is still present. Affinal relationships provide hospitality when traveling through unfriendly areas, helping assuage this element of fear. A person still does not venture through an alien area without having allies with whom to stay.

The complexity of affinal relationships naturally involves a certain amount of overlap between a person and various kin groups. In fact the more ways he can trace his relationship to a given kin group the stronger his bond or alliance will be. When someone has the option of choosing how he relates to another individual, he will choose the consanguineal over the affinal relationship. Occasionally he can manipulate his kinship ties for establishing a claim to land, goods, or personal friendship.

Any male is in a taboo relationship with his male affines. He is forbidden to call any of these persons directly by name, but uses euphemisms to either call or refer to them. Early in our study we were slow to understand this relationship or the responsibility of it. Someone would refer to an individual as "man" or "he" and we would press him to identify the referent. Whispering, he would say the name, being very cautious that no one would hear him. The taboo relationship (amou) is very close and strong in spite of such restrictions. Such persons share goods and services, and the relationship is a good source of bride wealth.

Friend Relationships

A third way to establish a relationship is as a friend. The mechanism is used to extend relationships beyond consanguineal and affinal ties, and is not limited by language or culture. People who share this relationship are called nati which roughly translates "friend" (wantok in Tok Pisin).[3]

The function of the nati relationship is fourfold: to establish hospitality relationships, open up the possibility of sister exchange, develop trading partnerships, and cement alliances. A development of one of these functions is that of extension of hospitality in distant communities. In traveling through areas for trading or visiting, one must have friendly homes in

3. The language helpers we have brought to the SIL center at Ukarumpa have formed nati relationships with other Sepik people, friends at the center with whom they are able to relate.

which to stay. If an individual's parents have no ties in a particular area, he may establish *nati* relationships and come under the protection and care of his *nati*. A *nati* relationship carries with it definite obligations of hospitality and friendship (Townsend 1969:152–53).

Spirit-World Relationships

Beyond relationships of the Saniyo-Hiyowe with living people, another important network of relationships is that with the spirits. Basically there are two kinds of spirits, ancestral and bush spirits.

Ancestral spirits are those of kinsmen who have died. When a person dies, his spirit (or shadow) leaves the body and flies or moves around near his village. The fear of dying outside one's own area is very great. If a person were to die outside this familiar area, his spirit would not be able to find the way back to its hamlet. Although I have not been told the consequences of an ancestral spirit not returning to its area, the idea is unthinkable for the Saniyo-Hiyowe. A young child was once brought to us with third-degree burns all over his back and side. We treated the child with the little medicine we had and kept him alive for a week. We then had the opportunity to send him and his parents to the hospital at Wewak. They agreed to go, but during the night they changed their minds and left the village for their own hamlet. We heard later that the child died two days after they left. It was unthinkable to them that he might die away from home.

During the first several days after a death, there is intense mourning on the part of close kin, with a longer period of mourning for immediate relatives. These outward signs of mourning demonstrate to the dead person's spirit the sincerity of the survivors.

Mourning taboos are placed on widows, widowers, and parents of children who have died. These taboos serve to placate a dead person's spirit. During the mourning period an individual is restricted from processing sago or hunting. This period varies in length from a month for distantly related kin to one to two years for immediate kin.

During the first period of mourning a widow eats only at night. She is completely covered with mud and secluded from men in the corner of a house near a hearth. She leaves her seclusion only after dark, accompanied by another woman. She is not to see or be seen by any man during this secluded period which corresponds to the cycle of the moon. Her head is completely shaven, and her dress is a particularly long ankle-length skirt. She is not allowed to hear her given name, but is referred to as "the widow."

At the time of the new moon, the first of a series of feasts occurs which is to appease the spirit of the deceased. At this feast the widow is released from her seclusion and avoidance of visual contact with men. This feast also releases more distant kin from the taboos which were imposed on them. Men generally try to kill a wild pig for the feast, but, depending on what game is available, they may have to resort to other types of meat. In one instance they were only able to secure sago grubs. Taboos placed on the widow restricting her food and work continue for up to two years. At this time a second feast is celebrated, releasing her from the taboos. She is then eligible to remarry.

If the spirit of the deceased is not convinced of the sincerity of his relatives, he will cause sickness and even death to the offending parties. There is no "natural" illness to the Saniyo-Hiyowe. All illness is caused by offending either a bush spirit or an ancestral spirit, or by the work of a sorcerer. Illness places restrictions on a person. A sick person is immediately placed on a taboo-based diet and a shaman is brought in to identify the spirit causing the illness. After identifying the spirit, the shaman prescribes certain taboos and sacrifices designed to appease it. The shaman also often ascertains whether or not a taboo has been broken. In the case of death by sorcery, the spirit of the deceased indicates to the shaman who was responsible and what action must be taken. On the other hand, a properly placated ancestral spirit can help his kin in hunts, warn of approaching danger, and tell when visitors are approaching the village.

Relationships during life affect how ancestral spirits treat their living relatives. A widow can be attacked by her husband's spirit for neglect in life, for marrying too soon after his death, for being unfaithful, or for just being a lazy wife. Knowing this gives the woman the incentive to be a good wife and a productive worker for her husband.

The Saniyo-Hiyowe also sense a close relationship with bush spirits. Taboos that affect this relationship are predominant in the minds of people. Most, if not all, bush spirits are considered evil. *Tapiye ipari* dwell in rock formations, *me ipari* dwell in certain trees, and *sa'i ipari* dwell in the river, streams, and ponds. Taboos connected with each of these spirits involve trespassing into their territory without appropriate ritual, indiscriminately whacking or cutting a tree where a spirit lives, or angering a spirit in some way. The ways a spirit is angered are not clear even to the Saniyo-Hiyowe. It is only later that they realize a particular spirit is angered, and a shaman is called to identify the spirit and the causes of his anger. The appropriate ritual can then be prescribed.

Conclusion

The Saniyo-Hiyowe society is characterized by a taboo system functioning in conjunction with the kinship system to control the behavior of individuals within the society. While kinship is the cohesive agent that ties the society together, the taboo system operates within it to lend solidarity to the society.

The three major factors of life which taboos cover, i.e., food, personal relationships, and the spirit world, control the Saniyo-Hiyowe society as people interrelate within consanguineal, affinal, friend, and spirit-world relationships.

References

Mayers, Marvin K. 1978. "The Basic Values: An Introductory Manual." (Field Manual Series, vol. 1: Cognitive Styles). Dallas, Texas: SIL

Meigs, Anna S. 1984. *Food, Sex, and Pollution: A New Guinea Religion.* New Brunswick, New Jersey: Rutgers University Press.

Radcliffe-Brown, A.R. 1952. *Structure and Function in Primitive Society.* London: Cohen and West.

Townsend, P.K.W. 1969. *Subsistence and Social Organization in a New Guinea Society.* Ann Arbor, Michigan: University Microfilms.

Feasts: Celebration or Obligation?

Judy Kennedy

Introduction

Feasts are a time of great celebration in the Kala Lagaw society of Saibai Island,[1] but these feasts also involve the fulfilling of extensive obligations that produce stress in significant areas of the culture. Feasts are common on Saibai. In fact, it is rare for more than three or four weeks to pass without a feast. Because of this frequency of occurrence it is important to understand the function of the feast in order to better understand the culture. The purpose of this study is to present both the positive and the stress-producing effects of Kala Lagaw feasts and the probable outcome if present trends continue.

The Torres Strait Islands, of which Saibai Island is a part, have been written about extensively through the years. The earliest extensive records are from the 1840s. One is a report by Brierly about Barbara Thompson who was stranded for several years on the island of Muralag (Moore 1979). At the turn of the century Rivers, in the *Reports of the Cambridge Anthropological Expedition to Torres Straits* (Haddon and Rivers 1904 and 1908), wrote an extensive ethnographic account of the culture. Beckett (1978), whose main research was done from 1958 to 1961, has written numerous articles on politics, marriage, and adoption in the Torres Straits. Recent research has been done by Helen Duncan (1974) in the area of economics.

---

1. This paper is based on field research by Rod and Judy Kennedy under the auspices of the Summer Institute of Linguistics from 1976 to 1981. Judy Kennedy contributed the content of the paper and was assisted in writing by Martha Wade.

Kinds of Feasts

On Saibai Island there are basically two kinds of feasts, distinguishable by whether or not invitations are required. Open feasts do not require special invitations; participation of the whole community is expected. Closed feasts are only for those who are invited, usually the extended family. Both open and closed feasts, however, have many elements in common.

Common Elements

The most common elements of feasts are food, decorations, dancing, and the participation of the church. These elements are not necessarily all present at each feast and the form in which they appear may vary, but the greater the importance of the feast, the more elements will be in evidence.

Foods for feasts are generally a combination of Western and traditional. Western foods include rice, tinned vegetables, tinned fruits, cakes, biscuits, candy, jelly, custard, and tinned cream. Traditional foods include dishes of yam or sweet potato and cassava in coconut. The meat (turtle, dugong, fish, or deer) is normally caught by the men. If no game is caught, then frozen chicken or beef is purchased from the store, or the feast is postponed.

Like food, decorations are a combination of Western and traditional. Western decorations may include raffia streamers, crepe-paper streamers, balloons, and ribbons. Traditional decorations are local greenery such as ferns, coconut branches, green branches from mangrove trees, colored seaweed, and banana plants. For most feasts these decorations are concentrated in a temporary shelter set up as an eating place.

Church participation in one form or another is present at most feasts. This participation may simply involve the priest saying a prayer before the eating begins, or a church service or mass held earlier in the day. Some feasts center around an event of the church calendar. Other feasts center on the active participation of the priest as he is blessing a person or a new acquisition.

Dancing usually comes after the meal is over, though it may be more central. The style of dancing may be either traditional or disco. For any important feast the traditional singing and dancing is practiced for weeks beforehand.

Open Feasts

Most of the open feasts occur on a yearly cycle since they are celebrating events in the Anglican church calendar. Other open feasts celebrate special events or are used for fund raising. They are for the entire community and do not require a special invitation.

The feasts celebrating events of the church calendar are interspersed throughout the year. These feasts vary greatly in the amount of community participation. Following a major feast, such as Christmas, there tends to be a clustering of smaller, more informal feasts. This clustering is a natural outcome of the fact that the families are already together for the major feast and the decorations have already been made.

Special events that are commemorated with feasts include such things as the archbishop's visit, the arrival of an important government official, or the unveiling of a monument commemorating an event in the community's history. Most of the community will participate in these feasts.

Fund-raising feasts are a distinct variation of open feasts. The whole community may come, but participation is limited to those who are willing to pay. These feasts are normally sponsored by a particular group such as the school, Mother's Union, or Sunday school in order to raise funds for projects. Fund-raising dinners are common; in these often locally caught game is used. Another is a "bring-and-buy," but this has an additional distinctive feature in that the food is not necessarily eaten at that time. In this latter type, other fund-raising games take place at the same time.

Figure 1 shows the various open feasts as they occur throughout the year. The estimated amount of community participation in each feast is indicated on a scale of one (least) to four (most). The most important feasts have a participation level of four.

Closed Feasts

Closed feasts center around rites of passage and the blessing of new acquisitions of members of the family. They are only for those who receive an invitation, which may be sent by word of mouth if it goes only to the close family or may be handwritten or duplicated if sent to the entire village. The number of feasts that a family holds, and the number of people invited, is directly proportional to the family's wealth and prestige.

On Saibai Island there are many feasts centering around rites of passage. They include infant baptism, baby's first birthday, child's first haircut, birthdays, first shave, engagement, wedding, funeral, arrival of a tombstone, and tombstone opening. There are also closed feasts for the blessing of the new house, dinghy, or outboard motor.

CYCLIC		Level of Participation				
		0	1	2	3	4

January:	New Year	
	Rem. of Decorations	
March:	Mothering Sunday	
April:	Easter	
	Rem. of Decorations	
	Anzac Day	
May:	Ascension Sunday	
June:	Holy Trinity Sunday	
	Rem. of Decorations	
July:	Coming of the Light	
August:	Church Bazaar	
October:	St. Michael's/All Angels	
November:	Mother's Union Break-Up	
Decmber:	Church Anniversary	
	School Break-Up	
	Christmas	
	Boxing Day	

NON-CYCLIC

Bishop's Visit	
Important Gov't. Visitors	
Turtle Supper	
Bring and Buy	
Disco	
Unveiling of Monument	

Figure 1. Levels of Participation in Open Feasts

Distinguishing features of closed feasts include gifts and the kind of food eaten. Gifts, which are not present in open feasts, are given to the honored person, the priest, or the church. The gifts range most frequently from $6.25 to $25.00. The food at closed feasts may vary from a simple afternoon tea to a full evening meal. If it is a full meal, then the meat may be pig, which is normally eaten only at closed feasts. When a pig is donated to an open feast, then it raises the prestige of the donor.

Figure 2 shows the minimal and maximal levels of involvement in each closed feast. Table 1 summarizes several features that distinguish closed feasts from open feasts.

PARTICIPANTS									Many Outside Relatives*
								Some Outside Relatives	
							Whole Village		
					Close Relatives +1				
				Close Relatives					
			Ext. Family						
		Nuclear Family							

FEASTS										

Infant Baptism

First Birthday

First Haircut

First Shave

21st Birthday

Birthday (+Wealth, Prestige)

Outboard, Dinghy Blessing

House Dedication

Engagement

Marriage

Death

Funeral

Tombstone Arrival

Tombstone Opening

Some Possessions Burned

──── Maximal Participation

━ ━ ━ Minimal Participation

* "Outside Relatives" are those living in other communities.

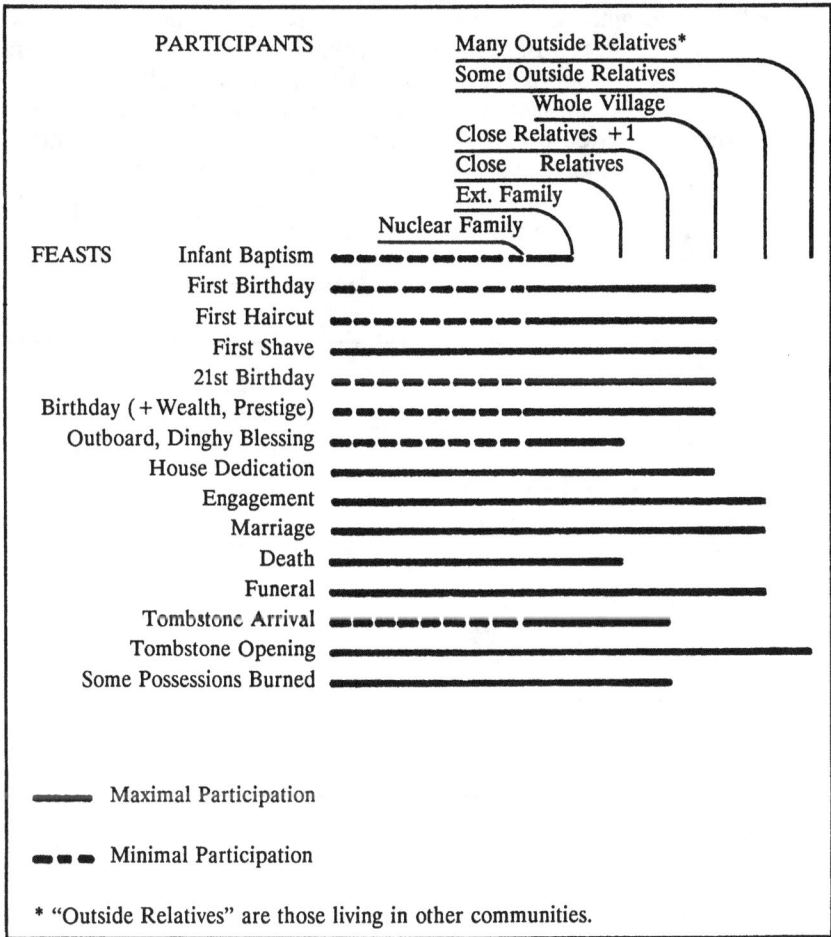

Figure 2. Participants at Closed Feasts

A Tombstone Opening

Tombstone opening is an event peculiar to the Torres Strait, seemingly
originating from the burial customs of the last century. Before missionary
contact the body of a dead person was placed on a *sik,* a special platform
above ground. Here the body would lie for some months until the head
fell from it. If the skin had dried hard and leathery, then people would be
confident that things were going well with the person's spirit, but if there
were more obvious signs of putrefaction people would be fearful that the
spirit would be troublesome. After the skull fell from the body it would be

polished, colored with various pigments, and used as an important object in divination and sorcery. Barbara Thompson, a castaway for several years in the Torres Strait, reports that while a skull was being cleaned, she was rebuked for screwing up her nose at the smell. She was told that she was insulting the spirit (Moore 1979). Apart from taking the skull, a few other bones would be taken and placed in bundles which were worn around the neck of relatives. These bundles were closely associated with hunting magic as well as protection from supernatural harm.

Table 1. Distinguishing Features of Feasts

	Open	Closed
Food	+	+
Dancing	+	+
Decorations	+	+
Church Participation	+	+
Possible fund-raising	+	−
Yearly cycle occurrence	+	−
Coordinated with Church calendar	+	−
Open to entire community	+	−
Rites of passage observed	−	+
Blessing of purchases	−	+
Invitation required	−	+
Eating of pigs	−	+
Gifts	−	+

When the head fell from the body, the platform and the body were buried together. A feast was held at this time. According to Barbara Thompson (Moore 1979) this feast, and the making of the charms with the various bones, marked the end of mourning for the deceased. Thompson speaks of a wife of a man from another island wanting to return to her home so that she could get some of her father's bones and end her mourning for him. Sinnika Turpeinen and Lillian Fleischmann (n.d.) write of the Bine people of southern Papua New Guinea who live geographically close to the Torres Strait people and who have a similar custom. A widow must take particular precautions until her mourning is ended. At that time her husband's spirit is said to go to its resting place, and she is then released from many taboos and becomes free to remarry.

The Pacific Island mission teachers of the London Missionary Society directed their converts to bury the deceased in deep graves, and today this practice is universal in the Torres Strait. The bodies are never allowed to remain above ground on the home island for more than one night. Tremendous effort and expense is made to ensure that the body is brought back to the home island if a death occurs elsewhere, and all will be in readiness to hold the funeral when the body finally arrives. A feast is held after the funeral.

The family then saves until they have money to buy a personalized tombstone. Large concrete surrounds are built for the grave. These are covered with tiles and the total cost comes to several hundred dollars. When a tombstone is brought in by boat the family may hold a small feast. They then continue to save to be able to produce a lavish feast at the time of the tombstone's unveiling. The men of the family work to finish preparing the grave site, the concrete surround is built, the headstone is set in place, and all the tiling is completed. All this time the headstone is kept wrapped in material and will remain so for some months after the gravesite has been completed and until the unveiling takes place.

Staging a tombstone opening involves a great deal of expense for the family, as they must cater for the whole community and many visitors. Costs are incurred for elaborate decorations, large amounts of food, and the charter of planes or boats to bring relatives from other communities —causing the total cost to rise to several thousand dollars.

At the formal ceremony a priest of the church, usually an islander, officiates. People make a procession to the highly decorated grave where the priest recites the virtues of the person who has died. He says prayers and sprinkles holy water, and then a ceremonial ribbon is cut. Protocol is very strict, and each act must be performed by a person in the correct relationship with the deceased. The feast that follows is larger and more elaborate than any other. Great efforts are made to bring in foods not normally seen in the outer islands, including fresh salad vegetables and freezer foods such as ice cream.

Positive Values

Feasts are central in the lives of the Saibai Islanders. These feasts, which involve large amounts of money, time and effort, provide the people with a sense of fulfillment in many areas of their lives. Some of the positive values of the feasts are now examined as they relate to family involvement, use of free time, competition for social acceptance, and the need for celebration.

Family Involvement

Feasts bring families back together and strengthen family relations by comforting the bereaved and by allowing the family to work together in planning and preparing for a big event. Family members, even those living and working far away, are expected to come to important feasts such as a funeral or a tombstone opening. This is true even when they have to pay air fares of $500.

Family relations are strengthened at the time of a funeral feast. Relatives come and stay until the funeral with the immediate family of the deceased. After the funeral some relatives may stay as long as a month with the family, especially if a young person has died. During this time the relative will comfort the immediate family and show that they are united with the family in their mourning.

In earlier times families worked together in gardens and in providing for other daily needs. Due to various social factors discussed below, it is no longer necessary to spend extended periods of time together in the garden. Feasts fill this need for family involvement by providing activities which allow them to work and plan together toward a common goal. Many young girls working in Cairns become homesick due to missing the involvement of planning and working together for a feast.

Free Time

Saibai Islanders now have much more free time than previously, due to social welfare benefits and the presence of a store. The planning and preparation of feasts provides them with a meaningful way of using new-found free time and money.

As citizens of Australia the people qualify for Commonwealth social services such as old age pension, child endowment, unemployment benefits, unmarried mother's allowance, and widow's pension. In addition they also receive free medical benefits and free air or sea transport for high school students. All these benefits have led to an increased cash flow.

With money and the presence of a store, the Saibai Islanders are able to purchase food when needed. This, too, has led to less time spent in gardening and hunting, leaving them with more free time. The Islanders have chosen to use this extra money and time for feasts that benefit large groups of people and draw them together in unity.

Competition

In addition to uniting people, feasts encourage competition and allow the people as a group to maintain a standard they feel proud of in the presence of outsiders. Families endeavor to show their wealth and prestige by giving more and better feasts than another family. There is also competition for prestige between groups in open feasts for fund raising. This is especially true in the annual church bazaar where members of clans will purchase any remaining items being sold by their own clan so that they can raise more money for the church than another clan and thus gain prestige.

When important visitors come to Saibai they are welcomed with a large feast prepared by the community. These feasts give the Islanders assurance that they have entertained well. Individual families are reticent to have visitors in their homes because they feel that they cannot provide sufficiently for the important visitors. As a group, however, they are able to prepare food that will honor their guests.

Celebration

Feasts provide periods of celebration and exhilaration in what might otherwise be a dull existence. These celebrations embellish their lives with colorful decorations, opportunities for wearing new clothes, eating of delicacies, listening to good music, and participating in dancing. During feasts people relax and sit around talking about past events. A special interest at these times is the discussion of past feasts and the quality of food at those feasts.

Through feasts, family relationships are strengthened, free time is used in a way that is meaningful to the group, individuals are able to demonstrate good citizenship and gain social acceptance by contributing to the community feasts, and there is a welcome respite from the ordinary day-to-day routine. Without feasts there would be a sense of void in various aspects of the lives of the Saibai Islanders.

Obligations

In addition to being times of celebration and social involvement, feasts are means of fulfilling obligations to both the church and the family. The present pattern of feasts is being reinforced because of the sanctioning presence of the priest at the feasts and the fear of retribution if obligations are not fulfilled through feasts.

Church

Obligations to the church include finances, providing for the priest, and the appeasing of God. The people are expected to raise funds and contribute to such financial obligations as the church assessment, church rebuilding fund, church project (such as a generator), and to take care of Mother's Union fees and the sending of a delegate to the Mother's Union Conference. There are weekly offerings at the church, but these tend to be very small. So the money necessary for meeting obligations to the church is raised through open feasts that charge for the food eaten, through the annual church bazaar at which food and other items are sold, and through gifts to the church which are donated at various closed feasts. Most of their financial obligations to the church are fulfilled through the annual church bazaar at which about $5000 is usually raised.

The people's obligation to the priest is technically met through the paying of the church assessment, a set sum of over $3500 a year which covers parish running costs including the priest's stipend and is administered by the diocese. Even though it is not unusual for the church to be up to three years behind in payment of this assessment, they have nevertheless raised comparatively large sums of money for more tangible projects. The system of church assessment is a relatively abstract notion. Because of this the people tend to set aside their responsibility for the church assessment; on the other hand, however, a priest working in his home area will receive gifts of money at closed feasts. The people also feel some obligation to share game and garden produce with the priest at other times. This more personal pattern of giving relates more directly to their own view of reciprocity and fulfilling obligations.

Feasts also fulfill obligations to appease God. By helping to prepare food and by donating food and money for the feasts, the people are fulfilling church requirements as well as obligations to God. Another means of fulfilling obligations and appeasing God is by the feasts given at funerals. At these funeral feasts the relatives attempt to persuade the spirits of dead people to be helpful. It is imperative that the people serve the spirit of the person who has died. If the spirits are pleased with the feast, they may go to God and act as mediators on behalf of the people in order to appease God.

Family

Obligations to family are fulfilled through reciprocal relations—good things are done for others so that they will be obligated to reciprocate at another time. Feasts are a special time for fulfilling and building up obligations with both the dead and the living.

The most important obligations are to those who are dying or have just died. If these people are treated well then their spirits will go to God and obtain benefits for them. The spirit of a dead person who is not appeased may cause many difficulties. An example of the type of social pressure tending to magnify this trend is the manner in which specialists in supernatural communication will tell a dead person's relatives that the spirit is not satisfied with the treatment he or she has received. The relatives may be told, for instance, that the temporary shelter over a new grave is not good enough. As a consequence, every relative is expected to contribute to the funeral and tombstone opening.

Obligations with the living must also be fulfilled or built up. By contributing to a feast, relatives are reciprocating for help on a previous feast, showing gratitude for acting as a mediator on one's behalf, or fulfilling one's obligations as godparents of a child. Contributing to feasts is also a means of building up obligations toward the contributor. If a person has contributed to many feasts, then when it is time for his own feasts, many people will be obligated to help and the feast will be big.

Sanction and Retribution

The church is seen to sanction feasts by its presence and its need for money. The present pattern of feasts is likely to continue due to the sanctioning presence of the church, the fear of retribution by family and church, and the fulfilling of obligations through the feasts.

The church is present in all aspects of life from birth to death. See Beckett (1978) for an historical perspective on the development of overall church involvement in community affairs. At each major event the priest plays a significant role. Since his presence is necessary for all major life events, and major events are always connected with feasts, the priest will be present at most major feasts. His presence and activity shows his sanction and approval of all things that are involved with feasts. Thus, feasts must be good and worthwhile.

To understand the church's dominance in feasts it is necessary to look at its emergence as a dynamic force in the community. Thompson reports that feasts were held in the 1800s, but they were eaten before dark and celebrated such things as victory in battle (Moore 1979). The following extract from the Tongan anthropologist Sione Latukfu explains how the

South Sea Island missionaries introduced a different concept of feasting to Melanesia. It became a dynamic alternative to war and the gaining of prestige through collecting the skulls of enemies. There was a radical change from eating in private to eating without fear in public.

> Feasting was also used by the South Sea Island missionaries to bring together people who had been hostile or traditional enemies. Informants said that while the European missionaries only visited the village occasionally and in a rather formal manner, the South Sea islanders would sit down with them, share betel nuts, and discuss their problems. Local people who happened to be in a South Sea Islands missionary's house at mealtime were invited to share the meal with the family. Gradually the South Sea Islands missionaries introduced the concept of feasts to mark important occasions and invited people to participate in them. When I visited Munda in the Solomon Islands in 1968, a feast was held, and during one of the speeches, the speaker pointed to me and said that it was the Tongans who had introduced this type of feasting. He imitated the traditional way of eating: people hiding themselves and eating furtively, looking around nervously to see whether anyone was watching them and waiting to attack or procure food remains to prepare sorcery against them. After the Tongans had introduced the new way of feasting, everyone sat together, even those who had been traditional enemies, and enjoyed a well-prepared meal without fear of attack. At Tonu, in Southern Bougainville, the people told of Taani Palavi, a Tongan missionary who had prepared a feast soon after his arrival and invited all the people to partake of it. According to their account, it was the first time in the history of Tonu that men and women had eaten a meal together in public. The following Christmas the people of Tonu prepared a big feast under Taani Palavi's direction, and he invited the leaders of the Roman Catholic faction in the area, with whom the Methodists had not been on speaking terms, to participate. Feasting Polynesian style has now become traditional throughout these areas of Melanesia (Latukfu 1978: 102–3).

In this way feasts have become inextricably bound up with the Torres Strait Islanders' version of Christianity and it is hard for Islanders to perceive of Christianity without feasts. Non-Islander churchmen on the other hand tend to view feasting as an interesting adjunct to worship, not as an integral part of the whole.

The church's need for money also reinforces the present pattern of feasts. Individuals find it difficult to give large weekly donations, but when the contribution will also provide nutritional food, a time of celebration, and the opportunity to fulfill obligations or gain prestige, then people are willing to contribute.

Another factor reinforcing the present patten of feasts is the fear of retribution from priest and family. If drinking, which the priest disapproves of, is suggested for a feast, then he may threaten not to come to a feast. If he is not present, the feasts for infant baptism, marriage, funeral, tombstone opening, blessing of house, and blessing of outboard and dinghy cannot be begun. His presence is rarely if ever withheld, but the threat of this would be a strong motivation for people to maintain good relationships with the church by good standards of behavior and by participating in church functions. This kind of power in the hands of priests is now declining however, leaving behind a degree of moral confusion. If a community is without a priest for a long time deacons assume many of the functions of a priest. During a priest's short absence people prefer to postpone many events until his return.

The fear of retribution from family also motivates the continuation of participation in feasts. This fear is seen in those who live away from home. Unless a person has made regular contributions to feasts the person is afraid or ashamed to go home. When returning home the person will be sure to give a large contribution for a feast. There is also fear of retribution from the spirits of those who have died. If adequate feasts are not given on the dead person's behalf, then his spirit may not go to rest in the world of the dead and may cause much trouble in this world. Many common misadventures are blamed on a spirit which is not satisfied, and there is a great fear that an unsatisfied spirit will steal the spirit of a sick person during sleep.

It has been shown above that feasts are more than celebrations. They are necessary for fulfilling obligations to the church, such as raising money for various funds, providing for the needs of the priest, and appeasing God. Obligations to the family are also fulfilled or built up by contributing to feasts. Since obligations to the family are built on reciprocal relationships, an individual will always be in the process of either giving or receiving assistance from another family member. Thus, feasts in their present forms are likely to continue due do the church's historic connection with feasting and the fear of retribution from family and church if obligations are not met in feasts.

Stress

Feasts are a time of celebration, but in their present form are producing cultural stress due to their size and quantity. This stress is becoming evident in postponing marriage, in the lack of development on the islands, and in the relationship between educated workers and their families. It is also possible to see how stress could develop between the church and the people.

Marriage

The necessity of celebrating each major life event with a feast, along with the fact that tombstone opening feasts are so expensive, mean that marriages often have to be postponed. Obligations to the dead are always given priority over those to the living because of the difficulties that the spirit of a dead person can cause. Thus young people who would like to be married are often told to wait until after an upcoming tombstone opening because the cost of providing for a wedding feast might delay fulfilling obligations to a deceased person. This may mean a wait of one or two years for young people.

The required feasts, the lack of housing, the custom of eldest child marrying first, the breakdown of sister exchange, and the consequent fear of parents not being cared for in old age, have all caused stress that has pushed the age of marriage for women to thirty years or more. With the rise of the marriage age there is a corresponding rise in illegitimate births and elopement, neither of which are socially accepted.

Economic Development

The great amount of money and time spent on feasts has contributed to the lack of development on the islands. The minimum cost of store-bought food for an important open feast, not including meat, is about $190. With a minimum of eight important feasts a year, at least $1500 a year is being spent on open feasts.

Important closed feasts have similar costs as well as the cost of numerous cash gifts to church, priest, and relatives. An estimated cost of one funeral was $3700, and tombstone openings are more expensive than this since more people come. The annual church bazaar requires another $5000, while all smaller feasts require payment as well.

With these large amounts of money, time, and produce being spent on feasts, it is understandable that there is not much development of small businesses and other money-producing occupations. As a result, the major source of income on Saibai Island continues to be social welfare services, while the major expenditures are feasts. Feasts are not, of course, the only reason for lack of development, but neither do they encourage it.

Educated Young People

The rounds of feasts also produce stress between educated young people and their families. These educated young people are becoming a part of mainstream Australian culture, and yet to maintain their family ties they must give up their own financial security in order to send contributions back home. If they decide not to send contributions, or are unable to send them due to financial difficulties, they are ashamed and tend not to go back to see their families. In this way, feasts and the necessity of contributing to them are producing stress between generations.

Church

Stress is not yet evident between the people and the church, but it is easy to speculate as to how this could arise. As the younger people become more a part of the modern world, and desire to see progress and development, resentment may grow toward the church. Younger people might easily blame the church for the lack of money and time since most feasts and gifts are for the benefit of the church. Thus the relationship between the people and the church may be viewed as nonreciprocal, since the people continually do things for the church and they see no tangible evidence that the church is doing anything to improve the people's material well-being.

Conclusion

Feasts are an integral part of the Kala Lagaw culture of Saibai Island. As a time of celebration, feasts unite families and provide a meaningful use of free time and creativity. These same feasts, however, are producing stress in marriage and between generations, and are contributing to the lack of economic development. The results of this stress can be seen in increased illegitimate births and elopement, the breaking off of family ties, and an economy the main source of income of which is social welfare services. This stress is mainly due to the present size and quantity of feasts. The present pattern of feasts is continually reinforced by the sanctioning presence of the church and the fear of retribution if obligations are not fulfilled.

If the present trend of young people towards modernization continues, there may also be stress produced between the people and the church. The blame for lack of economic development may easily be attributed to the church since the church is reinforcing the continuation of the present pattern of feasts which limits time and money for economic development. It will be important for the church to analyze its role in the feasts, for example, its role in the tombstone opening which is a ceremony that appears to give priority to death at the expense of life. The role will affect the church's future influence on the people. Both the beneficial and the stress-producing effects of feasts will need to be carefully weighed.

References

Beckett, Jeremy R. 1978. "Mission, Church and Sect: Three Types of Religious Commitment in the Torres Strait Islands." In *Mission, Church, and Sect in Oceania*, ed. by James A. Boutillier, Daniel T. Hughes, and Sharon W. Tiffany. (Association for Social Anthropology in Oceania, Monograph 6) Ann Arbor, MI: Univ. of Michigan Press.

Duncan, Helen. 1974. *The Torres Strait Islanders,* Vol. 1, Socio-economic conditions in the Torres Strait: a survey of four reserve islands. Department of Economics, Research School of Pacific Studies, Australian National University, Canberra.

Haddon, A.C. and R.W. Rivers. 1904 and 1908. *The Reports of the Cambridge Anthropological Expedition to the Torres Straits,* Vols. 5 and 6. Cambridge, England.

Latukefu, Sione. 1978. "The Impact of South Sea Island Missionaries on Melanesia." In *Mission, Church, and Sect in Oceania,* ed. by James A. Boutillier, Daniel T. Hughes, and Sharon W. Tiffany. (Association for Social Anthropology in Oceania Monograph No. 6) Ann Arbor, MI: Univ. of Michigan Press.

Moore, David R. 1979. *Islanders and Aborigines at Cape York: an ethnographic reconstruction based on the 1848-1850 'Rattlesnake' journals of O.W. Brierly and information he obtained from Barbara Thompson.* (Australian Institute of Aboriginal Studies No. 3) Canberra: Australian Institute of Aboriginal Studies.

Turpeinen, Sinnika, and Lillian Fleischmann. n.d. "An Old Woman's People and How They Lived." MS in Summer Institute of Linguistics Library, Ukarumpa, Eastern Highlands, Papua New Guinea.

The Intermediary and Social Distance in Western Torres Strait

Rodney J. Kennedy

Introduction

The following study explores the role of the intermediary in preserving harmony within Torres Strait Islander Society. A dominant concern of the Islander is smooth interaction with the people around him. Therefore the role of the intermediary between individuals has great importance in the daily life of the people, since it enables them to maintain a nonconfrontational stance with nonintimates. The intermediary acts as an initial go-between in interactions between nonintimates preventing sudden accidental expression of sharply contrary wishes.

A detailed ethnography of the Torres Strait was completed by W.H. Rivers and other members of the Cambridge Expedition of 1901 (Haddon and Rivers 1904 and 1908). Jeremy Becket also has made extensive study of the social and political dynamics of the people of the area (1961, 1965, 1978). Margaret Mead in her study of the Arapesh people deals with trade friends, leadership, and transmission and sponsorship relationships (1970:68–90). Edward Schieffelin, writing on forces within a Papua New Guinea culture that serve to mediate interpersonal relationships, states, "for this simple non-literate society, where most people deeply share the same values and assumptions within a tightly integrated system of symbols, that poetic metaphor is most poignant and powerful which is couched in terms of those symbols which most widely mediate upon human relationships, identity, and other domains in cultural experience" (1979:127–28).

The Kala Lagaw of the Western Torres Strait is a society which is basically integrated around three types of groups—sibling, clan, and interclan. There is a tendency for people to be open to social interaction in sibling groups while guarding against personal vulnerability as more outsiders are involved (see table 1).

Table 1. Interaction of Kala Lagaw according to social grouping

Degree Of Interaction	Type of Group		
	Sibling	Clan	Village or Beyond
Committment to the common good	unlimited	unlimited	limited
Motives for acting for common good	to prove performance is acceptable	to fulfill reciprocal role requirements	specific recipro- city; to increase indebtedness
Willingness to expose person- ality through well-known initiatives to work or or learn	very willing	high status: very willing low status: cautious of infringing elders' status	high status, specialist mediator: willing all others: cautious of infringing upon specia- list's status
Willingness to be seen as taking innovative initiatives	very willing	very willing; high status sibling group: collectively willing	very willing; clan group: very willing

Sibling groups are noted for their intimacy of interaction. Anything which tends to keep siblings apart is seen as undesirable. They share freely in the exchange of goods within the sibling group. The group con- tains the mechanisms for individuals to work to fulfill any obligation that is posing a threat. Alternatively, they also provide the mechanisms for the individual to withdraw temporarily from the larger kinship group.

Clan groups are only a little less intimate than sibling groups. While there is much freedom to interact within clan groups, this is more limited than for sibling groups. Requirements for mediation exist where conditions for comfortable social interaction are critical. The society monitors reciprocity at this level through role-defined expectations.

Interclan groups maintain a much greater degree of social distance and depend on specific reciprocity as a social device to monitor exchange. Interactions at this level are more restricted. An intermediary is needed to facilitate a degree of interaction with people outside the clan.

While these groups do exist, this social structuring is never completely rigid. For example, people do have close relatives and friends in other clans. With some of these they tend to display sibling or clan behavior rather than interclan behavior. Today, a breakdown of interclan barriers is evident among more educated Islanders, where belonging to the same ethnic group is beginning to assume the functional equivalence of common clan membership.

The skill of an intermediary lies in reinforcing the tendency for people to share the same values and assumptions within a tightly integrated system. The need to encourage unity is fulfilled by close adherence to expected role behavior. The mediator filters interpersonal communications and influences the parties involved to express their views to each other within the context of their respective status-defined roles. There is much dependence on interpersonal mediation to accomplish transactions with outsiders and with persons perceived to be of higher rank.

There are times when the avoidance of confrontation may be either necessary or unnecessary. When it is necessary to avoid confrontation, an intermediary may or may not be required. An intermediary is of course not required when direct confrontation is acceptable.

Unacceptable Confrontation

Each of the following nine case studies focuses on the service of the mediator as a preserver of smooth interpersonal relations in the Kala Lagaw society.

Presence of Intermediary

The need for mediation arises in the following instances: (1) when serious business is involved (cases 1 and 2); (2) when the initiator is of lower rank than the person to whom the transaction is directed (cases 3 through 6); (3) when the parties are comparative strangers (case 7); (4) when previous interpersonal conflict has occurred between the parties (case 8); and (5) when there is the possibility of conflict of interest (case 9).

Serious business

When there is important business to transact, an intermediary is called in.

Case Study 1: Negotiation of a Marriage

Traditionally, A young man who is romantically interested in a girl but he may not tell her so directly. He is restricted to such indirect means as using love charms on his body. The young woman is also limited in direct communication and passes word to the young man that she likes him through one of her close friends. Since it is seen that their interest is mutual, the friend of the girl becomes an intermediary to arrange for the couple to meet secretly. When the young couple wishes to marry each goes to a close clan sibling of his or her parents, asking the relative to ask the parents to give favorable consideration to the union. (This practice was common as early as 1847 [Thompson 1979]). It then becomes the parents' prerogative to talk over the possible marriage with their child and if they are in agreement they will institute negotiations with their own siblings and with the parents of the other party.

It is significant that while young people speak very openly with parents about mundane matters, they do not initiate conversations about such important and potentially controversial matters as choice of a marriage partner. The use of an intermediary shields the young person from potential shame, since he or she will experience shame if the plan is openly repudiated. The use of the intermediary gives the couple the hope that the older relative will, through his personal relationship with the parents, gently persuade them to look favorably on the request. Interestingly enough, a younger sibling of the parents is just as likely to dissuade the parents from agreeing to the marriage as he is to encourage the arrangement.

Case Study 2: Bad News

When a relative dies while living in some other place, news will first be sent to his clan leader in his home village, who summons all the relatives, simply telling them that there is some bad news. After all the relatives have gathered, the clan leader begins to recite the good qualities of the deceased. He does not give his name until everyone has had ample opportunity to guess his identity. It is regarded as a very serious matter to break this protocol.

This custom is important because it avoids giving people a sudden shock. In addition to sadness at losing a relative, there are other reactions. Torres Strait people have an elaborate belief system concerning interaction with the spirits of departed relatives. The prescribed procedure of community leader serving as intermediary allows the group to adjust to their new relationship with this relative who now has spirit status.

Initiator of lower rank

Besides the need to avoid socially unacceptable confrontations, the dependence on intermediaries serves a positive social function. It clearly indicates a recognition of the status and role of the intermediary as well as that of the person he approaches. Paying honor promotes social cohesion, reinforcing the existing social structure.

Case Study 3: The Christian Enquirer and the Clergyman

A large number of people within a particular church were involved in a renewal movement fully supported and encouraged by the expatriate clergyman. One young man wanted to speak to this socially higher-ranking clergyman about his desire to have greater personal involvement in this movement. He was on good speaking terms with him; in fact he knew him quite well. Even so, he still chose to ask the clergyman's wife to mediate his request for her husband to grant him an interview. The clergyman found this somewhat unacceptable, fearing that the young man might be half-hearted about his desire for deeper involvement. Nevertheless, in this case, it would have been very difficult for the Islander to approach the clergyman directly.

Case Study 4: The Workman Who Took a Low Profile in His Job

Two white nursing sisters employed by the government to work in the Torres Strait were having maintenance difficulties with the small diesel-powered boat used to carry them to different islands to hold clinics. A young Islander who worked as a tractor driver and airstrip maintenance man was employed by the same government department as the sisters. Though he was a capable mechanic and generally an active, obliging person, he did not offer to help them. Finally I went to help. As I was cleaning up oil spilled on the boat, the young man came and asked me to see the island chairman on his behalf to ask him if it would be all right for him to help fix the boat.

At least three factors caused this man to use me as an intermediary. (1) He belonged to a different clan from the chairman; (2) Islanders are far more hesitant than whites about offering suggestions to a person which may infringe on the prerogatives of his official position; and (3) the young man was many years junior to the chairman. It is very probable that the young man would have approached the chairman directly had he belonged to the chairman's clan or one more closely associated with it; had his age status been higher; or had there been no expectation that the chairman would take the initiative.

Case Study 5: The Honored Teacher

A lecturer and his wife from the School of Australian Linguistics spent six weeks on Saibai Island. Previous to this they had had extended associations with several Saibai Island young people, and as the couple were skilled cross-cultural communicators, the Saibai Island students related to them closely when at the school near Darwin in the Northern Territory. Other casual evidence suggested that even the students who had never been to the school and were taking the first part of their course on Saibai Island were quite comfortable in the couple's presence. Notwithstanding this easy friendship, as long as I was there and helping to teach the linguistics course, students continually asked me to mediate all manner of minor academic business they needed to transact with the visiting lecturer.

Young people tend to work through an intermediary, even where there is little or no fear of speaking to the higher ranking person directly.

Case Study 6: The Indirect Borrowers

For many people whenever they want to borrow something from me, they neither come themselves nor send a written note. They always send a younger relative. Young adult males may send a female relative of their own age. Apparently it does not matter if the younger relative is more closely related to the person making the request or to the person receiving the request. My children are frequently asked to carry requests to me. Women frequently bring requests to my wife on their own behalf to ask me for various things.

Involvement with strangers

Dealing with strangers indicates another positive need for mediation. Islanders appear to encounter few difficulties in making straightforward purchases from strangers in a normal retail setting where role expectations are rigidly defined. However, they are very disturbed with encounters that entail more ambiguities.

Case Study 7: "A Very Good Friend at the Booking Office"

One of the Saibai Island leaders was planning to come to Darwin (over 1600 kilometers from Saibai) to work with us on language research. We were making travel plans and discussing whether he would travel alone or with us. Having previously travelled a similar distance to Brisbane, he had no fear of plane travel itself, but very considerable fear of having to make a flight connection in a city he had never visited before. He said that he had no fear at the small flight booking office in a nearby town, because the lady who always took care of his needs was his very good friend. Since that time the gentleman has travelled more and feels quite easy about approaching desk attendants at an airline terminal, now that he perceives their role behavior as predictable. He often acts as an intermediary for relatives in this type of situation.

There are considerable similarities between Islander reaction to a strange situation and the reaction of Westerners who may be very unfamiliar with airline travel arrangements. However, the essential difference between them lies in the greater tendency among Islanders to stress dependence on a chain of persons to achieve some end. The Westerner tends to stress the possession of more abstract information and generalized skills.

Previous interpersonal conflict

There is a tendency to rely on an intermediary when interpersonal conflict has previously taken place.

Case Study 8: A Father Angered

Approximately six months after we went to live in the islands, two young boys, ages seven and ten, took a builder's tape measure from our house and smashed it between two rocks. I became angry and insisted that the two boys come with me to their father, something I learned later to be contrary to cultural norms. The boys came very unwillingly and when we finally reached their father, he became extremely angry with me. As a result I did not try to pursue the matter further. That evening a cousin of the father visited me and after a great deal of very general but friendly preamble told me that it was his desire to fix up any trouble and that he and his family were sorry that his relative had expressed his anger toward me. The intermediary arranged for me to meet his relatives the next day near the intermediary's house. Since the conciliatory meeting which took place the next day, the father of the boys has always continued to be friendly toward me.

This was a case where the boys' father and I were guilty of moderately serious breaches of the local social code. I feel that I received fairly generous treatment because the church enjoys high prestige in the islands and as a translator I am associated with the church. Had I not enjoyed this prestige there would have been less concern to heal the breach quickly.

Conflict of interest

Whenever there is potential conflict of interest, there is need for the services of an intermediary. While this need is undoubtedly present in marriage negotiations today, it also arose when the first missionaries came to various parts of the Torres Strait. The significance of intermediaries in the introduction of Christianity and the acceptance of the first missionaries can be seen both historically and in the way that this history is reenacted each year. Islanders portray the highlights of the roles of various intermediaries.

Case Study 9: Friends of the Missionaries

Both oral and written histories tell how Jawai, a Mabuiag Island man, worked for European shell fishermen, then later came to live on Dauan Island. When the mission schooner of the London Missionary Society visited Dauan on 6 July 1873, they depended heavily on Jawai to ensure their peaceful acceptance. In the Dauan Islanders' annual reenactment of this scene, all the warriors are depicted as lying in wait in the men's house while Jawai ventures closer to the shore to see who the visitors are. Later he welcomes the visitors and barely manages to restrain the other warriors from attacking them. The Saibai reenactment is very similar. Jawai and a Saibai Island clan leader, Nadai, both feature prominently as the intermediaries who smoothed the way. On Boigu Island an oral version features *ipi pawd,* the traditional custom of lending a wife to a group of men of an opposing faction. They attacked the canoe bringing the party of Lifu Island missionaries, but then a Dauan man who had had contact with these warriors called out to them and persuaded them to negotiate and then lent them his second wife for the day. More than a hundred years of Christian teaching notwithstanding, the old men who told this story speak very highly of the man's action in establishing peace by lending his wife.

Lack of Intermediary

While the presence of an intermediary is essential in many instances of unacceptable confrontation, there are other such instances in which the intermediary is lacking. These include avoidance through either physical or referential means.

Physical avoidance

Case Study 10: The Man who did not See the Argument

Soon after we went to live on Saibai Island I was surprised to see a friend emerging from the swamp on his way to church. He explained to me that when he observed two men having an argument, he took a detour so that he would not see them.

Islanders are skilled at not being at a place where their presence could cause embarrassment.

Referential avoidance

Case Study 11: Specific Criticism Avoided

The dismissal of church on a Sunday morning and the Sunday afternoon meeting held once each month for about three hours are each opportunities for leaders to deliver speeches of admonition to the community. Young adults are usually denounced vigorously, while older people are denounced in more general and less forceful manner.

There is also a great deal of caution about being the first to offer criticism. At one such meeting there had been strong criticism of excessive drinking and drunkenness. After about an hour I stood up and ventured the opinion that the black marketing of alcohol was even more worthy of condemnation than individual weakness with respect to alcohol. Immediately after this the priest and several other church leaders expanded on these sentiments at considerable length.

I asked an Islander friend later why no one had previously mentioned black market selling of alcohol. I was told that the priest (also an

Islander) had to use indirect modes of reference, *adhiaw ya* 'outside talk', lest he insult people. The person responsible for the black marketing was a close relative of an important man in the village. In this particular case, however, a great many people were very displeased with his behavior and were on the verge of criticizing such behavior publicly, without actually mentioning his name.

This man's name was never mentioned in the meeting. It is moderately uncommon for young adults to be named in a public meeting by way of criticism of their behavior, but I have never heard a senior adult named in a public meeting by way of critical accusation. I have heard only one instance of a senior adult named by way of admission of responsibility as a result of accusation.

Islanders exercise much greater liberty than do Westerners in making general social criticisms. It is the role of one of the lay church elders to do this, although naming offenders is a much more serious matter. The attitudes and values exhibited by Islanders are different from those exhibited by many Westerners who hold strongly to the view that it is better to have open, rather than secret, expression of criticism. While critical rumors circulate freely in Kala Lagaw culture, these tend to provoke no public response unless some prestigious aggrieved party feels that he has been publicly offended.

Acceptable Confrontation

Examples given so far have been related to the use of the intermediary to maintain smooth interpersonal relations in social interaction and the avoidance of confrontation. This may be described as maintaining proper social distance. In order to produce a more balanced picture of the Kala Lagaw people, it is equally important to look at contrastive situations where it is not necessary to maintain social distance. For example, in the vast majority of day-to-day transactions, no mediation is required between parents and their children. In a similar way, some of the dynamics of Kala Lagaw society are presented in contrasting situations where social intimacy is emphasized.

Borrowing Within Family

Case Study 12: Direct Borrowers

Some people always ask me personally to lend them something, or else if they send a youngster to me with a message, it is always a polite note written by the older person. If, as is often the case, the person making the request has first seen me away from my house and made all necessary arrangements, then he may send a younger messenger without any written note. Most people who conduct requests in this way also give us unsolicited gifts from time to time. Their behavior is typical of close relationships; they always use appropriate kinship terms for themselves and myself whether the request comes by word of mouth or by letter, and they freely express pleasure for any help received.

The behavior of direct borrowers is in marked contrast to the behavior exhibited by the other group of borrowers (see case 6) whose behavior is more like that of people buying, selling, or receiving wages, never expressing overt pleasure at the time of the transaction.

People who borrow from me indirectly seem to consider themselves either not to be my close associates or to be of lower status than I am. They are nearly all women, younger men, or a few older men with whom I have not been closely associated. Those, on the other hand, who are careful to borrow only by direct request are mostly older men. But they also include two older women, both of whom stand in a mother relationship to me according to my adoption as well as those men of my own age or a little younger with whom I have a particularly close association as a clan brother.

It is important to compare and contrast the two patterns of mediated and unmediated borrowing behavior. Whereas mediated borrowing (see case 6) maintains social distance and is similar to a purchase or wage agreement, unmediated, or direct borrowing (see case 11) maintains social intimacy and is an expression of sharing between close associates.

Mediated borrowing behavior can further be compared with mediated behavior in general. In both kinds, the person of low status avoids the danger of direct confrontation with persons of higher status; requests by distant associates to borrow consumables is frequently refused; and the intermediary is supposedly unconcerned as to whether or not the request is granted. The difference between the two types of mediated behavior is seen in the tendency for the intermediary in the borrowing behavior to be of lower status than either of the parties, while in other behavior he is generally of higher status than the initiator.

Agemate Relationships

I will now describe various other examples of behavior between close associates (cases 13 through 16) and to contrast this with behavior in relationships where social distance is preserved (cases 17 through 19).

Cohesiveness within clans is a basic cultural value of great importance to the Kala Lagaw people. People of one clan tend to live in one locality, and in premission times each clan would live in its own separate hamlet. People feel strongly the need to patch up any quarrels between close relatives as quickly as possible. Relationships are especially close between age mates within a clan and closest of all between clan siblings of the same sex. This cohesiveness must be seen as having important survival value for the community. We may relate this cohesiveness to the obligatory absence of mediation between age mates. Intimate fellowship among young age mates tends to be accompanied with quite a lot of vigorous horseplay, but close fellowship between older groups of age mates is expressed in ways that reflect more mutual honor and respect.

Work

In many aspects of Torres Strait life people demonstrate a strong tendency to relate closely with age mates of their own clan and to relate only a little less closely to relatives senior or junior to themselves.

Case Study 13: Fettlers Gang

It is fairly common for a group of Islander clan brothers to all find employment in the same fettlers gang, maintaining railway lines as far away as Mount Isa in the far West of Queensland. These men will often comprise the entire gang. They tend to retain their traditional language even when separated from their home community for many years. These groups of workers have been highly regarded by their employers and have a reputation for coping well with the harsh climate.

When people work together on a common project such as repairing the church, the same people like to spend their evenings relaxing together around a fire. Even during the daytime family social and eating arrangements tend to surround the work activity, and work and recreation are mixed. The people who tend to form one group for this purpose are the same people who tend to act as a single group for exchange and mutual assistance purposes. The group tends to be one clan with all the males having the same totem, but various relatives such as sons-in-law may attach to the group. I have been told that until the time of the Second World War food gardening was performed by large family groups who worked and relaxed together in this way. The extent of food gardening declined sharply as soon as this practice dropped out. Of course, during the war most of the able-bodied young men were away and this trend has continued as young men seek outside cash employment, but clearly there are numbers who remain on the island but play no active part in food gardening.

Any task, however, which the young men attack with vim and gusto is almost invariably performed by a group of agemates and these tend to come from one clan. These tasks include outside employment, hunting, village projects, preparing small temporary shelters and decorating them for feasts. Though the trend is not quite so pronounced, women of the various age groups and older men also show a strong preference for working as a clan-based group of agemates. A frequent reason for working in these groupings is the preparation for the very large number of extended family and community feasts (J. Kennedy 1984).

Since people have come to depend more on social welfare payments and proportionately less on hunting and subsistence agriculture, it may well be that clan-based groups of agemates working together to prepare feasts fulfills part of the need for intraclan cohesiveness which used to be supplied by the social interaction involved in hunting and food gardening. Nevertheless, hunting and fishing are still relatively important clan activities. Cooperation by hunters is important as is sharing of the kill or the catch.

Competition

Case Study 14: A Boat Crew of Clan Brothers

Clan brothers tend to gravitate toward each other in employment, so that on a cargo boat in the Torres Strait it is very common to find many of the crewmen coming from one island and all close relatives. As boxes and cans of groceries are hurled from hand to hand during the unloading from ship's hold to dinghy, the pace is very rapid. Anyone who cannot catch flour tins as rapidly as they are thrown to him is made to feel a weakling. The number of dented flour cans arriving at the village food stores is clear evidence of the vigor of these competitions.

One can see further evidence of the intimacy of intraclan cohesiveness within one age group of the same sex by observing the manner in which agemates compete with each other as they work or hunt together. Whereas Western youth tend to compete to establish winners, Torres Strait youth tend to put pressure on each other by challenging each other to keep up with the others in the group. Interpersonal competition takes the form of numerous small competitions between pairs of individuals as is often the case with circuit racing through the world. Whereas the Westerner has a greater tendency to compete to achieve the temporary status of winner which he enjoys in relatively deliberate isolation, the Islander engages in a type of competition which is intensely interpersonal. He who finally emerges as the most prestigious within a group has related to each person within that group in numerous small encounters. The significance of this behavior among Torres Strait Islanders is that it occurs so frequently within a group of same sex agemates within a clan.

Relaxation

The tendency to be able to work well as a group of clan brothers or clan sisters appears to have application to other parts of the South Pacific.

Case Study 15: The Jovial Sugar Growers

Captain Louis Hope, the first to grow sugar cane commercially in Queensland, is said to have had above average success with labor relations and productivity on his plantation. His success is largely attributed to the carnival atmosphere he maintained in the work environment. Young workmen from the island would laugh and joke together and vie to see who could be the fastest to drive a steam plow to the end of a furrow.

This is very much the preferred work pattern for Islanders. While elders in the Western society may frown upon young Westerners who engage in the behavior of turning work into a kind of game, older Islanders, on the other hand, strongly commend the practice and remark that if young fellows are happy and in a joking mood, they will work well. Islanders have a strong dislike for working alone, and they often express sympathy for me if they see me doing any manual labor alone.

Exchange and giving

Another strong feature of agemate behavior within a clan or a functional clan is the great freedom of exchange and giving. Islanders seem to practice specific reciprocity among less intimate associates and a freer type of generalized reciprocity among very close associates. The very pattern of kinship structure lends itself to the discretionary extension of kin relationships to their practical limits under the circumstances. More clan sibling relationships may be developed if need arises. The children of one generation of male forebears on father's side and female forebears on mother's side are all regarded as siblings. R.W. Rivers explored how people defined "brothers" under this scheme. Since *tukuyap* is the Kala Lagaw word for siblings of the same sex, he asked men who they regarded as *tukuyap*. He found that if two people were by our reckoning third or fourth cousins and happened to have very few dealings with each other, then one could describe the other as "a little bit *tukuyap*," thus suggesting that a relationship is recognized as existing but as not having been developed (Haddon and Rivers 1904).

Case Study 16: Relatives Far Away

On a number of occasions I have offered to record short messages on cassette from Islanders who have been absent from home for a long time. I have visited them in mainland cities and would be able to carry the cassette to a brother or sister back in the Islands. Initially they refuse, protesting that they feel a little ashamed at having been away from their home area for so long and therefore somewhat ashamed to send a message. But then we usually show them pictures of people from their home island and of their relatives, the ones to whom they might want to send a recorded message. Those who initially declined the offer now express a strong desire to be reunited with relatives and ask to be able to record a message to their siblings after all. Relatives who have attended to kinship obligations in spite of great geographical separation show no hesitation about sending cassette messages, since cassette recorders have become a large part of Islander life and are not mysterious or frightening.

While people who have maintained social contact without interruption are all eager to send messages to each other via cassette or letter, there is an initial reluctance to do so on the part of those who have failed to maintain close contacts.

Whereas Islanders show a strong desire to draw relatives back to their traditional homes and are prepared to spend large amounts of money for fares if necessary, accounts are kept concerning the extent to which traditional obligations have been performed. People who have missed out on performing certain obligations lose status as a result. For example, relatives sometimes debate regarding who is to control a piece of land. I have heard one party say that because a potential clan leader was absent from the funeral of the previous clan leader, he failed to carry out certain duties. Therefore authority to distribute clan assets fell upon those who were present at the funeral and were the ones who now carried out duties which would have fallen to the one who was absent.

Social Errors

Case Study 17: Drunk in Public

If men become intoxicated they are apt to become argumentative. In semi-private situations there may be vigorous arguments, but in public this is rarely the case. The public drunk tends to resort to oratory and self-aggrandizement. It seems that publicly challenging the positions of others is viewed so seriously by Islanders that even intoxicated persons remember not to do this. Relatives of the intoxicated person try to lead him away as quietly as possible. Later they may have a great deal to say to him, but their first objective is to minimize any public scene.

Kala Lagaw people do not like to lose face in public and thereby be shown to be vulnerable. A great deal of respect is paid to persons and the roles ascribed to them, so people place a high priority on not publicly challenging each other's roles. The behavior of both the intoxicated person and his relatives fits this pattern.

Case Study 18: Mother-Daughter Conflict

When an Island girl took an evening stroll with a visiting workman, the girl's mother disapproved and whipped her around the legs with the nearest handy object. The daughter immediately ran away and spent three days with relatives at the other end of the village before returning home.

Within one family, if a higher status person is sufficiently annoyed, he will confront a younger person, but it is normal for the younger person to withdraw from the situation as quickly as socially possible.

Case Study 19: Members of the Girl's Friendly Society Criticized

A situation similar to that in case 18 arose involving a number of local girls with visiting workers. The older women (the Mothers' Union, an organization of the Anglican church) all gathered and required the members of the Girls Friendly Society (junior equivalent of the Mothers' Union) to gather before them to be publicly shamed for their behavior. No men were present. Some of the young women, especially those over thirty years old, and those who had received formal education beyond secondary school, tried to offer some sort of verbal defense. However, any of the younger women who tried to defend themselves were verbally attacked in the most virulent terms by the higher status, married women. The higher status women, those entitled to speak, made all manner of accusations. Even those single women who were not accused of anything reported later that they tended to be very fearful lest they be criticized and that they kept their eyes on the ground so as not to attract unfavorable attention. The young woman against whom most accusations were focused chose to leave the island for several months to live with relatives in another town.

Single women are accorded low status because they are unmarried. Any attempt on their part to answer criticism evokes more serious criticism than the original incident. Low status people, whose status is temporarily lower because of an incident, feel very distressed at open opposition of high status people. This is a natural corollary to the nonconfrontational, mediation culture of the Kala Lagaw.

High status people occasionally publicly criticize lower status people, causing them to feel strong shame and thus to withdraw. People also tend to withdraw from a community if they find themselves in strong conflict with the local chairman or if, in the eyes of the local community, they have been guilty of serious misconduct. Strong, open criticism rarely occurs. When it does, it usually involves higher status people criticizing their own lower status relatives and generally results in a degree of social withdrawal by the person criticized.

Conclusion

The Kala Lagaw society of the Western Torres Strait is characterized by the utilization of intermediaries whose role is to help preserve harmony within the society. The intermediary's skill lies in supporting deeply-shared values and assumptions within a tightly integrated system.

The Kala Lagaw people are aware of personal confrontation and of obligations that are a part of the confrontation process. There are times when it is very important to avoid interpersonal confrontation. Some of these times warrant the presence of an intermediary, while some do not. An intermediary is necessary when serious business is involved, when the initiator of a confrontation is of lower rank than the other party, or when conflict is involved. Intermediaries are not necessary if one can avoid interpersonal confrontation through mere physical or referential avoidance.

There are also times when interpersonal confrontation is acceptable. These include borrowing within the family, in agemate relationships, and in reprimands due to social errors.

The intermediary filters interpersonal communications and influences the parties involved to express their views to each other within the context of their respective status-defined roles.

Mediation is seen as a vital factor in the smooth running of many aspects of life. In Kala Lagaw society both mediated and nonmediated relationships contribute to effective social cohesion and to relieve tensions within the society.

References

Beckett, Jeremy R. 1961. "The Torres Strait Islands." *Current Affairs Bulletin* 29:3.

———. 1965. "Political Development in the Torres Strait Islands." *Human Organization* 24:2.

———. 1978. "Mission, Church and Sect: Three Types of Religious Commitment in the Torres Strait Islands." In *Mission, Church, and Sect in Oceania,* ed. by James A. Boutillier, Daniel T. Hughes, and Sharon W. Tiffany. (Association for Social Anthropology in Oceania, Monograph 6) Ann Arbor, MI: University of Michigan Press.

Boutillier, James A., Daniel T. Hughes, and Sharon W. Tiffany. 1978. *Mission, Church, and Sect in Oceania.* (Association for Social Anthropology in Oceania, Monograph 6.) Ann Arbor, MI: University of Michigan Press.

Haddon, A.C. and R.W. Rivers. 1904 and 1908. *The Reports of the Cambridge Anthropological Expedition to the Torres Straits,* Vols. 5 and 6. Cambridge, England.

Latukefu, Sione. 1978. "The Impact of South Sea Island Missionaries on Melanesia." In *Mission, Church, and Sect in Oceania*. ed. by James A. Boutillier, Daniel T. Hughes, and Sharon W. Tiffany. (Association for Social Anthropology in Oceania, Monograph 6) Ann Arbor, MI: Univ. of Michigan Press.

Mead, Margaret. 1971. *The Mountain Arapesh*, Vol. 3. New York: Natural History Press.

Moore, David R. 1979. *Islanders and Aborigines at Cape York: An Ethnographic Reconstruction Based on the 1848–1850 'Rattlesnake' Journals of O.W. Brierly and Information He Obtained from Barbara Thompson*. (Australian Institute of Aboriginal Studies No. 3) Canberra: Australian Institute of Aboriginal Studies.

Schieffelin, E.L. 1979. "Mediators as Metaphors." In *The Imagination of Reality*. by A.L. Becker, and A.A. Yengoyan, Norwood, New Jersey: Ablex, pp. 127–44.